D0886798

Patterns of Irony
in the
Fables
of
La Fontaine

Patterns of Irony
in the
Fables
of
La Fontaine

RICHARD DANNER

OHIO UNIVERSITY PRESS
ATHENS, OHIO
LONDON

Library of Congress Cataloging-in-Publication Data

Danner, Richard, 1941–
  Patterns of irony in the Fables of La Fontaine.

  Bibliography: p.
  Includes index.
  1. La Fontaine, Jean de, 1621–1695. Fables.
2. La Fontaine, Jean de, 1621–1695—Technique.
3. Irony in literature. 4. Fables, French—History and
criticism. I. Title.
PQ1808.D36 1985   841'.1   85-15536
ISBN 0-8214-0824-0

197936

For my parents

Contents

Preface

In recent decades the *Fables* of La Fontaine have become the object of an increasingly broad spectrum of critical commentary. Numerous perceptive and methodical scholars have been attempting to rescue La Fontaine the fabulist from a long tradition that had found poetic art less interesting than aphoristic elements, literary history, or biographical matters. Although La Fontaine's works remain less widely investigated than those of a number of his illustrious contemporaries, readers now have access to a fairly wide range of published options when deciding how to interpret the *Fables*. Despite their modest instructional roots, the *Fables* are complex enough to admit a multiplicity of competing (or mutually reinforcing) approaches, and one must welcome the array of viewpoints pleading for assent as critics patiently seek to identify the intrinsic properties of Lafontainian artistry. At the same time, when faced with choices, one often feels compelled to choose—a natural reaction in this case because the various exegetical perspectives concerning the *Fables* are not all equally cogent. The strongest ones, in my view, are those that exploit—imaginatively, coherently, and with methodological rigor—important features that are demonstrably present in the poetic texts (as opposed to elements the analysis of which depends at least partly on recourse to extrinsic information). My reading of the *Fables* has led me to conclude that irony is an indispensable key serving to unlock many portals of La Fontaine's artistic mind. As I began considering the processes and products of his ironic outlook, however, I quickly became aware that my contribution to the ongoing critical dialogue would be more confusing than enlightening unless I based my explorations of the *Fables* on the best theoretical thinking devoted to the subject of irony in literature.

Thus the central aim of this book is quite uncomplicated: to show in a systematic and theoretically valid way that irony is a vital and pervasive aspect of La Fontaine's manner in the *Fables*. These pages by no means constitute an exhaustive treatment of the topic, but they are, I believe, one forward step in a process that promises to bear much fruit if other researchers agree to pursue the fabulist's muse along similar paths.

In chapter I, I discuss what several critics have written about the poet's ironic attitude. Although a number of stimulating essays on this topic have been published, the term *irony* has often been employed with more enthusiasm than precision; indeed, La Fontaine's ironic spirit has been clad in so many costumes that one can never predict what kind of apparel it will be wearing next. In chapter II, relying heavily on the work of D. C. Muecke and Wayne C. Booth, I construct a detailed theoretical foundation for the term *irony* as it is used throughout this study, in an effort to confine the word to a manageable (as well as clear) frame of reference; thus, though readers may disagree with the definition wholly or in part, they will at least know what is meant when I write about La Fontaine's uses of irony. Chapter III is concerned with the endings of individual poems and with possible relationships between irony and didacticism in the *Fables*. Chapter IV deals with La Fontaine's utilization of prosodic and stylistic devices in the service of ironic ends. In chapter V, I explore certain problems of Lafontainian irony in relation to an issue, far from resolution, that has fascinated critics for many years: that of the architectural principles on which the *Fables* are founded. The brief conclusion is less a summary of findings than an invitation to others to use my analysis of La Fontaine's ironic vision as a catalyst in examining from their own vantage point additional aspects of the poet's resourceful irony-making.

I hope that this monograph will be of interest not only

to seventeenth-century specialists and to other teacher/ scholars involved in French and comparative literary studies but also to graduate and undergraduate students in literature. It is assumed that all readers of this study will possess at least a basic reading knowledge of French; therefore, quotations from primary and secondary sources written in French appear only in the original. (Italics have been added to passages quoted only if so indicated.)

This book has been a long time in preparation and my debts of gratitude are many. No list of acknowledgments, however extensive, would be adequate to ensure against embarrassing omissions. A seminar on La Fontaine taught at Indiana University by Professor Francis W. Gravit in the mid-1960s provided an excellent basis for future investigations. A classroom discussion with my graduate students at Ohio University in the fall of 1972 prompted my realization that "Le Loup et le chien" is not the straightforward fable I had imagined, thus leading to my first article on La Fontaine. I wish to thank the editors of the following journals for permission to republish material from essays of mine that they first printed (see the Selected Bibliography, under my name, for details of publication): *L'Esprit Créateur,* the *French Review, Kentucky Romance Quarterly,* and *Papers on French Seventeenth Century Literature.* Professors Philip A. Wadsworth and David Lee Rubin have in various ways helped me sharpen my thinking about the *Fables,* and I am thankful to both of them for encouraging my efforts. Ohio University has tangibly supported my study of La Fontaine by means of a reduced teaching load for research (spring 1975), a Faculty Fellowship Leave (winter 1980), and a Baker Fund Award (summer 1982). Joyce Mills has saved me considerable time and energy by expertly typing a clean draft of my manuscript. I would like to thank the editorial staff of the Ohio University Press, and especially Helen Gawthrop, for the diligent skill with which they have prepared the monograph for publication. Finally, and most important, I am grateful to my wife Mary for her active interest in this project, for her professional as well as personal companionship, and for the ironic sensibility we share.

I

Critical Views on Irony in the *Fables*

Numerous critics have been aware that irony is a striking and even dominant aspect of La Fontaine's manner in the *Fables*. Several meanings have been ascribed, however, to the ironic vision ostensibly expressed in this poetry, and one is reminded of Wayne C. Booth's remark that "irony has come to stand for so many things that we are in danger of losing it as a useful term altogether."[1] Happily this confused state of affairs did not prevent Booth from proceeding to write an original and important study of irony that will figure prominently in the next chapter.

Virtually everyone dealing with irony in literature would probably start by saying that it involves a conflict between what seems to be real and what is real. In other words, though it is doubtful that any two readers could ever reach complete agreement as to the meaning of irony in all its manifestations, one might well approach unanimous accord by contending that the ironic mode is always characterized by tension resulting from the contradiction of appearance by reality. But then it becomes necessary to define *appearance* and *reality*. Do these terms relate to truth and illusion in intrinsic literary contexts or can the concepts of what is real and what is apparent correspond to historical situations and events as well? On such points consensus has not been attained by scholars writing about irony in the *Fables* of La Fontaine.

The first scholar to examine Lafontainian irony, as

such, in some detail was Odette de Mourgues. Organizing her material according to the Horatian principle of
utile dulci (which became the formula *instruire et plaire* in
French neo-classical theory), she devoted a chapter of her
elegant study, *O Muse fuyante proie*, to "l'ironie poétique"
of La Fontaine, a subdivision in her view of the concept
plaire.[2] She approaches the topic by focusing on a certain
quality that

> implique de la part du poète la faculté de percevoir et
> d'exprimer un écart, un désaccord, entre, d'une part, le
> langage poétique dont il use et, de l'autre, la réalité qu'il
> suggère, si bien que le poème nous donnera nécessaire-
> ment une vision double et contrastée des choses. L'attitude
> du poète à l'égard du désaccord qu'il exprime varie suivant
> les cas: elle peut n'être que simple amusement, ou au con-
> traire indiquer une très sérieuse préoccupation. (*O Muse
> fuyante proie*, p. 132)

She says that the French language lacks a term to identify
this quality, whereas English literary critics, T. S. Eliot in
particular, describe it as wit. This is the quality that she
will call "ironie poétique." She continues by declaring
that this quality is not restricted to any country or period
and that it can appear in various forms. Though it might
be useful to distinguish between irony and wit, for the
present purposes it will suffice to assume that Odette de
Mourgues's "ironie poétique" is the equivalent of the English term (poetic) irony.

Few would quarrel with the main idea conveyed in the
foregoing definition: namely, that irony is generated by a
contrast between what is said and what is intended, between the surface meaning of poetic language and an underlying reality that contradicts it. However, this definition leaves a number of questions unanswered. Is the
locus of the correcting reality always in the text or may it
be sought elsewhere? Does the poet's "vision double et

contrastée des choses" destroy the surface meaning, or can it coexist with the reality that it implies? On what grounds will the reader decide whether the poet is addressing his subject with an amused or serious attitude? If the range of potential authorial stances is so broad, why, as de Mourgues maintains, is a writer unable to express poetic irony in more than a single tone? Are the attitudes the artist conveys those of the biographical author or of a literary persona (or both), and how can the reader know?

After relating her explanation of "ironie poétique" to the poetry of the *précieux* ("Toute poésie précieuse est, par définition, basée sur un désaccord, sur la rupture délibérée qu'établit le précieux entre l'univers convention-nel et rassurant de la société précieuse et le monde de la vie réelle," p. 132), de Mourgues indicates how the irony contained by such poetry differs from that of La Fontaine:

> Alors que dans le poème précieux, l'ironie poétique ne se sert de la réalité que pour faire ressortir encore plus toute la frivolité du contenu, La Fontaine se servira d'une ap-parente frivolité pour mettre en relief la réalité qu'il dépeint. Le poète précieux ne veut qu'amuser. Pour la Muse des *Fables* plaire et instruire sont inséparables. (pp. 135–36)

Not many readers would be likely to confuse a typical poem by La Fontaine with a piece by Benserade or Voi-ture, but it is hard to imagine how the level of *frivolité,* apparent or otherwise, could serve as a workable distin-guishing factor. The reconstructed *réalité* of an ironic fable of La Fontaine is not necessarily more instructive than its superficial meaning, nor is the surface of such a poem inevitably frivolous. And does the "apparente frivolité" apply to the viewpoint of the reader, that of the author, the narrator, or one or more characters? Finally, the poet's official pronouncements aside, do we have the impression when reading the *Fables* that much instruction is really being accomplished? Even if so (as Odette de Mourgues undertakes to demonstrate in her chapter entitled "Instruire," pp. 83–100), how are we to determine whether *instruire* is an integral part of La Fontaine's "ironie poétique" or an accompaniment that does not in itself contribute to the definition? De Mourgues offers a partial answer to this last question when she asserts, "L'ironie poétique sera pour La Fontaine, en même temps qu'un élément de charme, un instrument pour explorer son univers de moraliste" (p. 136), but one is left wondering precisely how the lesson-giver does the bidding of the ironist (or maybe the other way around).

After having discussed the poetic irony in a celebrated passage from *Adonis* ("Rien ne manque à Vénus . . ."), de Mourgues proceeds to discuss what she terms the same type of irony in the fable "Les Deux Pigeons."[3] In her judgment this is indeed a pervasive quality:

> Cette ironie poétique est présente partout dans les *Fables.* C'est en elle que nous percevons, comme étant inséparables, les deux sourires du moraliste: celui de l'intelligence et celui de la tendresse. C'est d'elle que le comique des *Fables* tire non seulement son unité mais aussi ses caractéristiques de subtilité et d'élégance. (p. 138)

Those familiar with the *Fables* may well react to these sentences with an impulse of vague recognition: unmistakably, these are Lafontainian traits mentioned by a sensitive scholar who knows her poet intimately. The problem with her comments, however, is that they do not measurably advance our awareness of irony in the *Fables* as a distinct phenomenon. Such notions as "sourires . . . de l'intelligence et . . . de la tendresse" or "subtilité" or "élégance" are simply too imprecise to be very helpful as identifying features.

At this point there seems to be a slight shift in terminology, with *comique* being substituted for *ironique* as a descriptive label, because in the next paragraph we read:

Toute vision comique semble, de par ses conventions
mêmes, impliquer une certaine sécheresse: simplification
du dessein pour que s'accuse toute l'absurdité d'une contradiction, isolement du personnage comique coupé du réel
ou du normal, détachement du spectateur à qui est interdit
tout mouvement profond de sympathie. (p. 138)

If the critic intends to incorporate irony into the comic
vision, it is unclear how one concept relates to the other.
Detachment of the spectator (or reader) is often considered a basic property of irony in literature. How can
we be sure, if this is judged to be the probable response
of an audience to a work or passage, whether the structure in question is ironic or comic or both?

De Mourgues goes ahead to state, in regard to the *Fables*, "quant au détachement du lecteur, il est assuré d'a-
vance puisque cet univers où parlent les poissons est de
pure fantaisie." It is true that readers of these poems are
likely to be struck by the incongruity of animals talking and
behaving as people do, but is the universe of the *Fables*
more fantastic (as a world of esthetic invention) than that
of *Phèdre* or *Madame Bovary* or any other novel, play, or
poem? Does fantasy necessarily produce detachment?
(My reaction to the recent science-fiction film *E.T.* was in
no way detached although extraterrestrial beings remain
—so far as we can tell—in the realm of the fantastic.) Is
every work with personified beasts ironic? It seems to me
that one of La Fontaine's principal accomplishments was
to *add* elements of irony to the traditional Aesopic apologue. To be sure, Odette de Mourgues's grasp of what
constitutes irony in the *Fables* is not limited to the simple
animal-as-human parallel (see, for instance, her illuminating discussions of "La Grenouille et le rat," IV, 11, and of
"Le Rat et l'huître," VIII, 9: pp. 139–41, 176–82). My quarrel is not with her exegetical skill but with her somewhat
casual handling of irony as a concept inadequately differ-
entiated from other stylistic and rhetorical features.

Commenting on these famous lines from "Les Animaux malades de la peste" (VII, 1) highlighted by their
unexpected *rime en écho,*

> Même il m'est arrivé quelquefois de manger
> Le Berger,

the critic writes: "Ici, comme en beaucoup d'autres endroits, l'ironie poétique exploite les ressources d'un langage qui ne souscrit pas aux fins utilitaires de cet autre
langage d'informations claires et distinctes qu'est la prose"
(pp. 143–44). This sentence raises more problems of theory
that would be difficult to resolve. Is prose a mode of
expression that will admit no ironic touches, or would such
irony have to be called *ironie prosaïque?* (Apparently not,
because in a note on p. 151 the critic asserts that Gérard
de Nerval's *Sylvie,* a work in prose, contains "une forme
d'ironie poétique atteignant un degré de perfection ex-
quise.") And to what *prose* is the critic referring—scientific, journalistic, everyday, literary, or all of these? If our
fabulist aims to instruct as he pleases, and if there is a
relationship between didactic intent and ironic vision, is
his language not directed in part to certain "fins utilitaires"? Or can we say that in the lines quoted above (as
well as in the "autres endroits" of similar thrust) the poet's lesson-giving self has been replaced by his purely artistic self? If so, when does he remove one of these hats in
order to don the other—and what clues allow us to be
certain?

   As will be suggested later in this study, an important
aspect of La Fontaine's ironic vision in the *Fables* is the
poet's refusal to adopt the kind of anthropocentric attitude toward his characters that human readers are conditioned to expect. Odette de Mourgues calls attention to
this lack of an ontological bias in the following passage:

> Avec une frivolité délibérée, La Fontaine se plaît à ignorer
> la hiérarchie sur laquelle repose pour nous l'ordonnance du
> monde, cette échelle des êtres qui va du minéral à la divi-
> nité, classification immuable qui place par ordre d'impor-
> tance croissante les choses inanimées, les végétaux, les ani-
> maux, les hommes et les dieux. Non seulement le poète
> substitue à cet ordre un autre ordre suivant lequel un pot
> de terre, une fourmi, une laitière, Phébus ou Borée sont
> tous des personnages d'égale importance, mais encore il
> introduit entre ces êtres des rapports qui, d'après notre
> jugement, ne sauraient exister. Ironie poétique de base, qui
> joue sur l'architecture même de tout cet univers poétique.
> (p. 146)

Selecting as the basis of my discussion a fable of metamorphosis, "Les Compagnons d'Ulysse" (XII, 1), I will
attempt to show that the principle enunciated here has
interesting implications for a general reinterpretation of
the *Fables*.

Finally, summarizing her discussion of the words
spoken by the fox in "Les Animaux malades de la peste,"
Odette de Mourgues appears to hint at the presence of a
technique to be considered later in this chapter, and elsewhere, under the term "Double Irony," though she does
not develop the notion sufficiently to permit full understanding of the double reality she intends:

> C'est peut-être une des plus belles réussites de l'ironie
> poétique que de pouvoir exprimer non seulement un déca-
> lage entre l'irréel et le réel, mais encore un contraste entre
> deux réalités dont l'une n'existe, semble-t-il, que par le
> pouvoir magique des mots. (p. 145)

Theoretical imprecision seems, as in other cases, to undermine this insight because any literary reality, in ironic
as well as in nonironic structures, ultimately exists only
"par le pouvoir magique des mots." Thus the boundaries
of the "ironie poétique" she is describing become blurred.

A somewhat different perspective on Lafontainian irony appears in an article by Jacques-Henri Périvier published in 1971.[4] This critic proposes, as one reason explaining why "la théorie de l'amoralité des *Fables* n'est vraie que d'une vérité *apparente*," that ". . . l'ironie de la plupart des fables trahit la présence d'un jugement subjectif et moral que le poète prononce contre tout ce qui n'est pas en harmonie avec sa vision mythique d'un monde idéal" (p. 335). One might ask by what internal or external code of ethics the poet's judgment is to be termed "moral," and also whether the designation *poète* refers to the person behind the work or the "implied author" (Wayne C. Booth's phrase) inside the work. These are not petty distinctions. Analysis of ironic structures in literature depends partly on making such determinations at the outset.

Like de Mourgues, Périvier indicates that instruction is an essential element of the fabulist's ironic approach, but he would presumably disagree with her contention that the ironist "ne saurait . . . chanter que sur un ton," for he writes:

> . . . c'est en suivant les chemins de l'ironie, tantôt faits d'arabesques légères, parfois de traits sarcastiques, que nous retrouvons dans les *Fables* de La Fontaine cette vision mythique que l'imagination du poète se fait de l'homme et du monde dont elle valorise négativement le mal. (p. 335)

What we do not have here is a mechanism for deciding whether a given light or bitter touch is in fact ironic.

Having declared that in the *Fables* La Fontaine typically poses as an objective observer of reality, Périvier states:

> Chez le fabuliste (comme chez Flaubert, par exemple) l'objectivité se vêt d'ironie. Or, l'objectivité de l'ironiste manque d'authenticité: c'est une feinte de moraliste. Il se peut que cette adresse subtile soit parfois interprétée comme le signe d'une indulgence plénière accordée aux

hommes par une intelligence sans illusion, mais nous croyons qu'elle recèle le plus souvent le jugement moral d'un
esprit courroucé. L'ironie relève de l'esprit de litote et con-
siste à dire le moins pour suggérer le plus: ici, à ne pas
blâmer pour mieux condamner. (p. 340)

My own reading of the *Fables* confirms that the veneer of
narrative impartiality often has an ironic hue, but I am
less willing to admit that authorial objectivity signals the
pretense of a moralist. In the course of this study I hope
to demonstrate that the irony of the *Fables* tends to be
incompatible with the notion of an "esprit courroucé"
condemning his adversaries by indirection. On the other
hand, "l'esprit de litote"—approached from a different angle—will be seen as an essential property of the fabulist's
ironicalness.

Périvier advances a fascinating interpretation of what is
ironic about the human-like animals in the *Fables:*

L'ironie réside même dans le choix qu'a fait le poète de
s'exprimer dans ce genre particulier qu'est la fable animale.
C'est que, dans les *Fables* de La Fontaine, aux exceptions
près, l'allégorie animale n'est pas le grossissement de la
nature humaine . . . ; elle ne traduit pas non plus un rapport
d'équivalence . . . ; l'animal est bien plutôt la représentation
euphémisée de l'homme. . . . Dans les *Fables*, cet esprit de
litote, intrinsèque à l'ironie, rejoint la pudeur euphémique
de l'esthétique classique. (pp. 340–41)

Though this thesis is a refreshing departure from anthropocentric perspectives founded on extraliterary criteria, one wonders whether it could be suitably applied to
most of the nonhuman characters in the *Fables*. Besides,
once the convention of personified animals has been
established (in the first poem of Book I), it quickly
becomes (in itself) a rather banal source of irony.

But Périvier's view of irony in the *Fables* is more complex than that. He asserts that not only the poet's "vision

démonique de l'homme," but also its opposite, "la vision également mythique de ce qu'il peut y avoir au coeur du poète de plus pur et de plus beau," can find expression by means of irony (p. 341). This interplay of contrary states causes irony in the *Fables* to be "un perpétuel démenti à elle-même." Périvier closes his article—and his discussion of La Fontaine's double attitude toward humankind—by offering the impression that "L'ironie est chez lui comme la lucidité du rêve" (p. 342). Such subjective language, lovely as it is, leaves the concept of irony in limbo.

A recent article by Roseann Runte features a more tightly controlled set of terms.[5] Runte is interested in analyzing "the dialogue which the narrator maintains with his reader" in the *Fables* (p. 389).[6] She considers the narrative strategies of the *Fables* to be quite complex:

> La Fontaine created a self-conscious narrator who fulfils several roles and functions. He is a heterodiegetic narrator who recounts a story in which he does not participate. He is also a homodiegetic narrator who relates a tale which he has witnessed or observed either in real life or in literature. (pp. 389–90)

She proceeds to isolate four separate functions assumed by her "homodiegetic narrator" and argues that "La Fontaine's particular art lies in the interrelation between the heterodiegetic and the homodiegetic narrators" (p. 390). As for the reader, he or she "enters the narrative on the level of the heterodiegetic narrator" and "is thus intradiegetic," whereas "the extradiegetic narratee is the virtual reader" (p. 392). According to Runte, "La Fontaine's extended system of dialogue between narrative personae and readers is unique" (p. 393). How do La Fontaine's fables differ from their sources? Whereas in the traditional fable "the author condescends to enlighten the reader," in those of La Fontaine "the reader condescends to join the poet in evaluating the allegorical relation and the moral as implied or stated." So it follows that "the Aesopian fable is straightforward while La Fontaine's is devious" (p. 394). A comparable distinction separates La Fontaine from his imitators, because "where La Fontaine is implicit, the eighteenth-century fabulist is explicit" (p. 396).

How do these findings confirm the "keys to irony" cited in Runte's title? She states:

> The structure and tone of La Fontaine's fables meet the conditions described by many critics as characteristic of irony. . . . La Fontaine's homodiegetic narrator, when filling the testimonial function, shows himself to be a naïve witness and when fulfilling the ideological function, he demonstrates the limits of his own understanding. In short, this narrator claims to be something less than he is in reality. He plays the role of an *eiron*. He understates, renounces exhaustiveness and places confidence in the reader to interpret and understand, to complete the textual implications. The text itself is elliptical rather than encyclopaedic. . . . The term irony can be applied to the "fusion in a spectator's mind of superior knowledge and detached sympathy." This surely is the effect created by La Fontaine's narrator. (pp. 397–98)

Much in this assessment is promising. In footnotes here and elsewhere in the article, Runte reveals her familiarity with a number of important theoreticians of irony, and her analysis gives evidence that she has reflected on certain problems of definition inevitably raised by the topic she is treating. Some of the concepts to which she refers will be developed in the next chapter.

Runte's analysis of narrators and readers in La Fontaine leads her to an explanation of how the poet creates what is commonly known as dramatic irony:

> In La Fontaine's fables there are the erring characters presented by the heterodiegetic narrator. They are judged

by the homodiegetic narrator and the extradiegetic narratee or virtual reader either agrees or disagrees with the
homodiegetic narrator. These roles parallel those which
are found in dramatic irony: the victim, the author and the
audience. In La Fontaine's fables the audience (the reader)
and the narrator collaborate to discover the victim. (p. 398)

This contention appears fundamentally valid, but the critic does not explain the process underlying her identification of dramatic irony in the *Fables.* Can we always be
sure, in reading this poetry, who the victim is? If so, what
kinds of clues produce this feeling of certainty? A similar
type of question-begging occurs in this assertion: "Another characteristic of irony is its manner of instruction. It
achieves its effect through pleasure" (p. 398). I do not
dispute Runte's claim that for our fabulist it is the *dulce*
that matters most (". . . La Fontaine concentrated on pleasure while the eighteenth-century fabulist considered en-
joyment to be secondary to instruction"), but such a declaration about a trait of irony, in order to be persuasive,
would have to include at least a minimal definition of
pleasure and suggestions as to how the reader can determine whether such an effect has been achieved in a given
poem.

Another aspect of irony in La Fontaine, according to
Runte, involves how his attitude toward content has been
interpreted:

The eighteenth-century fabulist failed to recognize the illusion which was deliberately created by La Fontaine.
When he spoke seriously of insignificant matters it was
ironic. The fabulists of the next century did not interpret
correctly the ironist's mask. They saw it as a true face.
They mistook appearance for reality. The result is the difference between La Fontaine and his successors. . . . La
Fontaine's pleasantries seem serious, while during the Enlightenment, what was serious was made to seem amusing. (pp. 398–99)

What Runte says about those who misunderstood the *Fables* could be applied as well to many twentieth-century readers (those, for instance, whose preoccupation with overt moral statements in this poetry is accompanied by a neglect of undercutting tone). However, I am puzzled by the claim that La Fontaine dealt with "insignificant matters." What explains this judgment? That many of his characters are nonhuman and thus of less consequence than people? This is the old anthropocentric bias informed by extraliterary considerations. That the *Fables* finally operate in a comic mode that is viewed—by tacit definition—as lacking the significance of tragedy or epic? If this belief is intended, it springs from a highly debatable standard of literary values.

In the following passage, Runte describes in her own way a process that almost any theoretician would ascribe to irony:

> Irony, in general terms, is the clash between connotative and denotative signs. The superficial text makes a statement which is counter to the implied meaning. To interpret such a text the reader must engage in a process of reconstruction. He must peer into the text and unmask the *eiron*. He must tear down the surface features and reconstruct meaning. The author invites the reader to form a new conclusion. La Fontaine, through his narrative personae, commences the process within the text itself. (p. 399)

In other words, appearances are deceiving in an ironic text. This is safe ground. In the next sentence, however, Runte creates an unexpected complication when she describes how La Fontaine develops the narrator-reader collaboration: "He dramatically engages with the reader in discovering the implications of the allegory." What causes trouble here is the reference to allegory. If allegory exists "when the events of a narrative obviously and continuously refer to another simultaneous structure of events or ideas . . . ,"[7] it would seem very unlikely that the *Fables* are allegorical in general (a case could perhaps be built for a few isolated poems), because we do not find obvious and continuous parallels between the action described and a second level of meaning (e.g., between any Lafontainian lion and Louis XIV). Furthermore, the notion of a different "simultaneous structure" implies that the surface and hidden levels coexist, whereas Runte contends that the reader has to "tear down" the former and "reconstruct" the latter. Such activity is no doubt incompatible with the nature of allegory. Wayne C. Booth, discussing the allegory of a passage from Bunyan's *Pilgrim's Progress*, notes: "the reconstructed meanings are added to, not subtracted from, what a strictly literal reading would yield" (*A Rhetoric of Irony*, p. 25). He proceeds to distinguish clearly between "stable irony" (to be discussed in my chapter II) and allegory:

> This distinction is not merely of theoretical importance. For the reader there could not be a greater difference between the traps laid by stable irony and the invitations offered by allegory. A naive reader who overlooks irony will totally misunderstand what is going on. A naive reader who reads an allegory without taking conscious thought, refusing all invitations to reconstruct general meanings out of the literal surface, will in effect obtain an experience something like what the allegory intends: the emotional and intellectual pattern will be in the direction of what it would be for the most sophisticated reader. (p. 25)

Booth does acknowledge the existence of the category of "ironic allegory," but it does not appear that Runte is referring to it when she talks about "the implications of the allegory" in the *Fables*. Whatever her meaning, she returns to the motif in her concluding paragraph:

La Fontaine socratically asked his reader to become a philosopher and discover both his own and the narrator's errors. The invitation is indicated by the tension between overt and covert significance and is delivered in the dialogue between authorial personae and reader which frames the allegorical narration. The double-tiered literary structure parallels the intellectual construction the reader will build by the juxtaposition of antipodal meanings. (p. 400)

Runte does not attempt to establish what might be the allegorical import of the *Fables*. Her final comment about the reader of this poetry (". . . La Fontaine's reader is conarrator, continuing the creative function in reconstructing in his own terms the significance of the fable," p. 400) seems a commonplace denoting the traditional role of the literary critic. If the meaning of any work were an unequivocal given there would be no need for interpretation. Happily such is not the case with La Fontaine. Disciplined reconstruction of meaning in the *Fables* is amply repaid. Roseann Runte's "keys to irony" do not unlock all its darkened portals, but her essay does represent a serious effort to grapple with meanings of a notoriously evasive rhetorical term. Despite some infelicitous phraseology (expressions like "extradiegetic narrratee" call too much attention to themselves but do not necessarily advance our understanding of the poetry under discussion), she partly succeeds in laying a theoretical foundation for some of the ironies at play in the *Fables*.

Yet another approach to the fabulist's irony is revealed in a recent essay by Carrol F. Coates.[8] This critic seeks to discover in the *Fables* the "meaningful interplay of various structures of sound, discourse, and images" (p. 62) said to characterize poetry in general. In the following paragraph, Coates explains how irony may be seen to underlie the coherently developed poetic texts to be discussed (works in which "no discernible structures can be assumed to be independent of or unrelated to other structures of the poem"):

> The framework which seems to permit the establishment of a meaningful relationship between La Fontaine's deviations from classical poetic practice and the sense of the fables is that of an overriding ironic vision of society and human behavior. (p. 62)

This general impression is explored with reference to these three "techniques of irony":

> First of all, the discrepancy between the use of classical rules of versification and deviation from these rules would seem to be one manifestation of the poet's global irony. A second technique is the ironic aside or intervention of the narrator, who repeatedly interrupts both the exemplary fable and the moral commentary on the narrative. Finally, there is an important ironic mode of discourse, called in French *discours indirect libre,* which will bear a brief commentary. (pp. 62–63)

The initial concept of "ironic vision" appears to float in a vacuum because theoretical underpinnings are absent. It is not expressly defined, nor do the three "techniques of irony" automatically affirm the poet's "overriding ironic vision of society and human behavior." Does the critic's discussion of these three techniques clarify their ironic basis?

As for the poet's use of *style indirect libre,* "Because it allows the narrator to assume the point of view of a character without subscribing to it, and to dissimulate his own judgments, it is an ironic mode of discourse" (p. 63). One can, however, easily imagine a character drawn with sympathy whose situation is nonetheless developed through the use of *discours indirect libre.* When, in portraying the woodcutter in the well-known fable "La Mort et le bûcheron" (I, 16), the narrator asks by means of an indirect strategy, "Quel plaisir a-t-il eu depuis qu'il est au monde?" (a question we can picture the character himself forming), the effect does not seem to be clearly ironic. Thus, free indirect discourse appears not to contribute, in itself, to a definition of irony.

Despite the interesting analyses of passages from "La Cigale et la fourmi"(I, 1), "La Cour du lion" (VII, 6), and "Le Corbeau et le renard" (I, 2), Coates's article does not adequately reinforce the hypothesis "that the ultimate sense of the meaningful relationship between poetic form and meaning lies in an understanding of La Fontaine's ironic view of the world" (p. 73) because the irony purportedly informing the poetic texts remains too fluid. Why is there a "level of irony," per se, in this opposition the critic perceives in "La Cigale et la fourmi": "the Cicada's joyous song expresses an esthetic perception of the world, while the Ant's sarcasm expresses a disdain for the Cicada's view and implies a practical perception" (p. 73)? It would appear that these juxtaposed viewpoints constitute the most straightforward element in the fable. And what, precisely, is ironic about the second level cited by Coates?

> The next level of irony is that of the narrator, who presents a dramatic conflict in which the *dénouement* is the Ant's refusal of the Cicada's request, signifying the irreconcilability of conflicting world views. (p. 73)

How does the narrative stance involve the reader in the razing and reconstruction of meaning? Is irony here another word for the plurality of potential responses? Earlier in the essay Coates had suggested

> that La Fontaine may have deliberately played a game with his readers by placing at the head of the *Fables* an ambivalent fable, leaving Louis XIV and other potential critics to infer a lesson of the triumph of industry over the

> pursuit of frivolous pastimes, when a very different inter-
> pretation is possible. (p. 63)

Coates may not be contending that irony and ambiguity
are interchangeable terms, but the lack of preliminary
definitions leaves the issue itself ambiguous.

Coates proposes the identification of "at least two levels of meaning in the ironic world view of La Fontaine"
(p. 73), those that Susan W. Tiefenbrun (whose analysis
of irony in the *Fables* will be treated next) has termed
"topical" and "universal."

> The topical level is that of the social and political world in
> which La Fontaine lived and to which at least some of the
> fables clearly allude. This is the world in which La Fon-
> taine's patron, the finance minister Foucquet, can find
> himself denounced by his rival, Colbert, and thrown into
> prison almost from one day to the next. (p. 73)

As Coates indicates, this dimension (in the 1668 collection: Books I–VI) has been extensively discussed by René
Jasinski.[9] For most modern readers this level of ostensible
meaning is so deeply hidden (even in passages where allu-
sive clues may invite such reconstruction) as to be virtually
irretrievable. Although Jasinski's erudition is admirable
(even awe-inspiring), searches for historical parallels tend
to trivialize literary texts, abandoning the esthetic for the
evanescent. On the other hand, irony, as conceived in the
present study, directly addresses the problem of artistic
worth. Besides, if the topical side of the *Fables* is almost
always obscure, it seems to lack a condition required for
the establishment of irony in a text: a mechanism permitting communication between the author/narrator and the
reader, allowing the latter to reject the surface meaning
and to comprehend the hidden meaning.

What, according to Coates, is the "universal" level of
irony operating in the *Fables?*

The other level is that of La Fontaine's understanding of the universal laws of human behavior, his perception of a world, including that of Aesop's times as well as that of Louis XIV, in which men continue to act like beasts or puppets rather than like rational and compassionate beings with the ability to discern treachery, to moderate desire, to perceive and respond to social needs. (pp. 73–74)

This assessment of the thematic significance of characters in the *Fables* differs markedly from Périvier's contention that the Lafontainian animal is "la représentation euphémisée de l'homme." Although the poet's comprehension of behavioral laws may have ironic elements, Coates does not provide a basis for determining exactly how such irony is generated. Does the notion of men behaving "like beasts or puppets" refer to such creatures outside literature or within? Whether or not one detects here a trace of extraliterary anthropocentrism, it is not clear why the motif of beastly conduct on the part of humans deserves (in the abstract) to be judged ironic.

In short, as a vehicle for systematic application of criteria of irony to the *Fables,* this essay by Carrol F. Coates leaves a good deal to be desired, though it does make other kinds of contributions to Lafontainian studies.

Susan W. Tiefenbrun, in her buoyant essay on irony in the *Fables,* confronts the problem somewhat more systematically.[10] For Tiefenbrun, "Irony involves the art of the hidden, the elusive, the oblique" (p. 144). She wisely chooses to simplify conventional enumerations or typologies:

Classical rhetoricians distinguished several varieties of irony which I prefer to call signs of the one technique whose structural model involves the simultaneous juxtaposition of mutually exclusive oppositions, a synthesis of dissonances, and the surface fusion of disquieting contrasts. (p. 144)

Although the oppositional element of irony is presumably beyond argument, whatever definition of terms one may decide to adopt, it is not clear at this point whether the hidden sense is to be subtracted from or added to the surface meaning. Does the critic elucidate this matter in the following passage (which immediately follows the sentence quoted above)?

> Double or multiple meaning and the disparity between statement and intention normally associated with irony are results of this synthesis and interplay of connotations, more accurately described in semiotic terms as an intersection of metaphoric codes. (p. 144)

The notions of multiplicity of meanings, interplay, and synthesis (additive) appear to conflict with that of a "disparity between statement and intention" (subtractive), but the critic seems to favor the latter when, citing functions of the verbs *chanter* and *danser* in "La Cigale et la fourmi," she analyzes the ironic effect of sarcasm ("where what is said is the exact opposite of what is meant"). Tiefenbrun goes on, moreover, to assert: "The litotes or understatement, whose signs say less than they signify, is the essence of irony" (p. 145). While this figure can be seen to have additive properties (Chimène's "Va, je ne te hais point" in *Le Cid*, III, 4, means literally that and considerably more), this is not what Tiefenbrun intends; illustrating her argument with reference to the famous lines "La Fourmi n'est pas prêteuse; / C'est là son moindre défaut" (I, 1), she contends that the poet "says the opposite of what he means and thereby creates not only the ambiguity of irony but the extension of meaning characteristic of evocative poetic discourse" (p. 145). Are these lines really ambiguous, however (three centuries of dispute notwithstanding), if the fabulist's hidden meaning can be confidently discerned? And is the relationship between irony and ambiguity so stable, so widely recognized, that it can be convincingly stated without demonstration?

Having noted, with regard to litotes, that "its rhetorical counterpart is the hyperbole whose amplified signs say more than they actually signify" (p. 145), Tiefenbrun is careful to explain that the mere presence of either figure does not automatically create irony:

> A disparity between what is stated and what 'is,' or what is meant, is the necessary contrastive mechanism underlying irony. Thus all hyperboles or litotes are not automatically ironic; the classification system is more complex. An identification of a structural mechanism of contradiction must precede for the typology to be justified. (p. 146)

Thus the oppositional quality of any ironic structure, now more clearly subtractive, remains fundamental.

Another "binary pattern" revealing irony in the *Fables* is conveyed by recourse to paradox:

> Since irony involves the simultaneous expression of two meanings, it is the perfect vehicle for the depiction of nature's paradoxical reality. It is no surprise, then, that the oxymoron and paradox *per se* are common rhetorical signs of ironic intention. And whenever the writer creates an illusion, especially of beauty, and suddenly destroys that illusion by a change of tone involving a reversal and contradiction, a surprising ironic effect is achieved. (pp. 148–49)

Here as elsewhere, Tiefenbrun reinforces her theoretical statements by referring to individual poems (the central focus of her analysis is Book I).

In the following passage, while reiterating her basic position, Tiefenbrun joins the critics for whom the communication between author/narrator and reader is of primary importance:

> When there is juxtaposition and equation of disparate elements, or when an identity is created between at least two opposed if not contradictory structures, the resultant incompatibility or contradiction is called an ironic effect. . . . The reader is an essential factor in the dialectical process for unless he perceives the relationship existing between a minimum of two equal and opposite elements of meaning, the incongruity is virtually inoperative, and the ironic effect is absent. (p. 150)

The idea expressed in the final sentence, no doubt widely acknowledged, suggests a broader truth about literature that must be kept in mind: the success of any work—ironic or not—depends on its being understood by an informed, sensitive reader. As for irony, it cannot be comprehended by any reader unless the author has provided adequately explicit signposts. It is always essential to begin by searching for the signposts (elements that appear ironic according to a predetermined definition). To assume that the work is ironic and then to search for supporting evidence presents the risk of reductionism and other forms of misreading.

Here we find Tiefenbrun apparently starting at the hypothetical level:

> That irony is essentially an oppositional structure is borne out in the fables if we consider merely the titles in the first book. Invariably two speakers, two ideas, two moralities are juxtaposed in a contrastive frame and in a symbolic language of allegory which is, in itself, contrasted to the direct language of the narrator's moral appearing usually at the end or at the beginning of the fable. (pp. 150–51)

Although I am willing to accept that every ironic structure is in one way or another oppositional, it does not follow that every opposition in literature must be ironic. To be sure, in her essay Tiefenbrun does make many astute comments about ironic elements in the *Fables*, but in the first sentence of the passage just cited she seems to begin with the assumption of prevailing irony, then to use the argument concerning contrastive titles as evidence, ipso facto, in support of her thesis. Do such titles as "Le Rat de ville et le rat des champs" (I, 9) or "Le Loup et l'agneau" (I, 10) reveal in themselves "a disparity between what is stated and . . . what is meant"—Tiefenbrun's "necessary contrastive mechanism underlying irony"? While such titles are indisputably oppositional, it is not obvious under what conditions the "binary pattern" thus created will become subtractive. And can we be certain that a poem's "contrastive frame" is in fact ironic if the author uses "a symbolic language of allegory"? Soon she elaborates by relating irony to allegory as follows:

> What is common to the fable, the allegory, and the satire is the necessary presence of hidden elements, messages concealed within a symbolic system that requires decoding and translation. Irony is, like language itself, an allegory for it says one thing and means another, is not meant to be believed but understood, and its symbols require interpretation for successful communication. (p. 152)

At issue here is not the existence of hidden features but what happens to the surface elements after concealed elements are disclosed. If irony "says one thing and means another," would it not be more accurate to describe allegory as a figure that says one thing, hides another—and means both? The confusion stems in part from Tiefenbrun's decision (judging from references in her essay) to rely principally on Vladimir Jankélévitch. Though his book, *L'Ironie*,[11] should be read by anyone interested in the subject, his analysis, however sagacious and thought-provoking, is finally too dispersive and impressionistic to serve as a comprehensive theoretical model. Like Tiefenbrun (who refers to the following sentence), Jankélévitch assimilates irony to allegory: "L'ironie pourrait s'appeler, au sens propre du mot, une *allégorie,* . . . car elle pense une chose et, à sa manière, en dit une autre" (p. 42).

Tiefenbrun, following Jankélévitch, adds *alterity* to her stock of oppositional terms ("Alterity is the essence of irony's deceptive powers by which surface language expresses the exact opposite of its intended meaning," p. 153—*plus ça change.* . .), quoting with approval his rather mystifying account of the matter:

> Entre les possibles que l'intelligence lui donne à choisir, l'ironie choisit l'altérité la plus aiguë: elle exprime non pas quelque chose d'autre que ce qu'elle pense, comme n'importe quelle allégorie, mais le contraire, qui est l'autre le plus autre; l'extrêmement-autre. Et elle est *antégorie* en cela. Elle va d'un extrême à l'extrême opposé de cet extrême, c'est-à-dire *a contrario ad contrarium.* (*L'Ironie,* p. 71)

It is not made clear how the earlier assimilation of rhetorical terms is to be reconciled with this attempt to distinguish irony from "n'importe quelle allégorie."

In the final analysis, the gains of Susan Tiefenbrun's essay on the level of explication are to a degree offset by the loss of sufficient exactness in her definition of the controlling term, irony. On balance this may ultimately be a small defect, but for my present purposes it is crucial.

Jules Brody's published reaction to Tiefenbrun's analysis (see note 10 above) raises other issues that deserve brief mention. Although he compliments Tiefenbrun on being one of the few critics who have "dare[d] come face to face with La Fontaine's use of language," Brody maintains that "she delivers only as much as she can cram into the undersized and somewhat antiquated structuralist van" (p. 77). Whereas, he contends, Tiefenbrun "craves objective structures," La Fontaine can elude such an approach "because along with structure, and often in place of structure, he gives us texture" (pp. 77–78). Unlike Tiefenbrun, who views "the thematics of alterity" in the *Fa-*

bles as "the enemy of familiarity and expectation" (p. 159), Brody discerns predictability in repetitive surprise effects:

> When plants and animals always speak human language, when unexpected reversals always occur, when ambiguity and paradox are always present, when binarity, in a word, is so recurrent as to be predictable, is it possible to talk meaningfully of *antiphrastic models* emerging in *reversal of expectation*, or of ironic effects being actualized *contrary to expectation*? Or, in more pointed terms, are such models the stuff of deep or merely surface structure? (pp. 78–79)

Proceeding to answer his own questions, Brody argues that from the "mature reader's" perspective, "the reversal model in La Fontaine, because it is recurrent and ubiquitous, obtains not contrary *to* but in fulfilment *of* expectation" and that for such an alert *archilecteur* "the structural pattern of La Fontaine's typical fable is about as unpredictable as the dénouement of *Hamlet*" (p. 79). I cannot imagine anyone henceforth examining Lafontainian irony without confronting these basic issues. With regular maintenance the "structuralist van" will not become outmoded for a long, long time, but binary structures may be as prevalent in a comic strip or a pulp-magazine fictional piece as in a fable of La Fontaine, yet it is unlikely that all of them inhabit the same esthetic dwelling. In other words, it is imperative that my analysis of irony in the *Fables* go well beyond an identification of hidden, oppositional ironic structures to a consideration of what is artistically valuable in such structures. Implicit in this will be a rationale for bothering to write this book in the first place. If this mission is not to be an empty exercise in literary scholarship, I must be able to persuade someone —somewhere—that irony is an element that makes the *Fables* worth reading. (Susan Tiefenbrun would surely agree; whatever my reservations about aspects of her definition of irony, her informed, impassioned readings of the *Fables* demonstrate, as she says, how it is possible "to find satisfying and serious intellection amidst the joys of light-hearted comedy," p. 159.) To convince anyone that irony in La Fontaine has esthetic value, it will be necessary to move above (or beneath) structure. As Jules Brody states, aligning himself with Jean Rousset, "The work is no more the sum of its structures than the forest is the sum of its trees" (p. 79). His abandonment of structure and advocacy of texture ("Beneath the structure, in the texture, is where the *action* is," p. 80) are justified in theoretical terms when he writes:

> Decipher the code and you get the message; decipher conflicting or intersecting codes and you get mixed, paradoxical, ambiguous messages. The trouble is that poetic discourse shuns discursiveness. It should not mean but be. Its essential function is not message, but massage, not the communication of meaning, even multiple meaning, but the creation and manipulation of multiple attitudes *towards* meaning. (p. 81)

Such luminous thinking about literature, put into practice, can help to shift the balance that for much too long favored nonesthetic issues concerning La Fontaine ("Le fabuliste est-il ce qu'il semble être?") or moral, philosophical, thematic, or sociological preoccupations ("Les *Fables* doivent signifier au lieu d'être"). When Brody converts theory to explication, in his discriminating "textural" reading (to be discussed later) of "Le Loup et le chien" (I, 5), he joins a growing band of Lafontainian critics whose implicit motto could be the poet's declaration that "Les Fables ne sont pas ce qu'elles semblent être" (*F*, VI, 1). What interests Brody in the writing of La Fontaine and his contemporaries is "the poeticization of the prosaic"; thus the critic summarizes his discussion of "Le Loup et le chien" ("a random choice" in the poet's large storehouse of fables) by contending that

> the irony, or the poetry of doubleness and duplicity, has its roots not in the intersection of metaphoric codes but in the deconstruction of rhetorical modes, in the weaving together of opaque discursive, previously invented lexical elements in a poetic fabric. (p. 87)

To probe, synthesize, and supersede the "opaque discursive" materials constituting the *superficie trompeuse* of the *Fables:* this ideal *modus operandi* will guide me in the chapters to follow, being utilized with as little imperfection and as much success as my struggling exegetical powers can muster.

My exploration of the ironic texture of the *Fables* will have as one of its aims a better understanding of the particularity of La Fontaine's literary art:

> When binarity and its variants are invoked as the major sign of poetic efficiency, it is predictable that the same explication will be written for all texts by sophisticated, complex writers. This seems to be the inescapable fate of all formalisms. There are just not enough particular forms and structures available to accommodate the annoying variety and uniqueness of literary talents and artistic performances. (Brody, p. 87)

But even before launching a discussion of the variety, singleness, and esthetic value of ironic devices in the *Fables,* I need to be reasonably certain that the elements under examination are ironic. It will therefore be essential to base my reading of the *Fables* on the most comprehensive, rigorous, and accurate theoretical analyses of irony currently available.

The two "ironologists" whose work I have found to be the most helpful are Wayne C. Booth and D. C. Muecke.[12]

These two theoreticians provide the conceptual foundation underlying David Lee Rubin's excellent essay on "double irony" in the *Fables*.[13] To avoid repetition, at this point I will refrain from discussing Rubin's treatment of theories advanced by Muecke and by Booth, because issues of this kind will be fully aired in the next chapter. Let it suffice for now to say that Rubin's approach is especially promising because he clearly recognizes the speculative complexities inherently related to his topic and because, acting on this awareness, he engages in careful, informative literary analysis from a position of theoretical clarity and coherence. This is the only sensible way to deal with a problem involving the use of a slippery rhetorical term, as I realized when drafting an article on irony in the *Fables* that was published several years ago.[14] I am convinced that, though we surely disagree on various issues, in these essays Rubin and I were both on the right track, moving toward our objectives with safe, deliberate speed. In neither case, however, was enough distance covered to enable us to reach our destination. The journey amid thickets of theory to the heart of Lafontainian irony is long and hazardous. Now, in the company of some enlightened traveling companions, I propose to cover a wide stretch of this picturesque territory, though it be fraught with pitfalls.

NOTES

1. *A Rhetoric of Irony* (Chicago: Univ. of Chicago Press, 1974), p. 2.
2. *O Muse, fuyante proie . . . : Essai sur la poésie de La Fontaine* (Paris: José Corti, 1962), pp. 131–51. See also her shorter study, in English, *La Fontaine: Fables* (London: Edward Arnold, 1960), especially the sections on "Tenderness and irony" in chap. 2 and on "Wit" in chap. 3.

3. Unless otherwise noted, references to La Fontaine's *Fables choisies mises en vers* throughout this study are taken from the edition prepared by Georges Couton (Paris: Garnier, 1962). Other editions of La Fontaine's works being used herein are: *Contes et nouvelles*, ed. Georges Couton (Paris: Garnier, 1961); *Oeuvres diverses*, ed. Pierre Clarac, Bibliothèque de la Pléiade (Paris: Gallimard, 1958). These editions will be abbreviated, respectively, *F, C,* and *OD,* unless the context makes obvious which work is being quoted. References to individual fables will give book and poem numbers in that order (for instance, "Les Deux Pigeons": IX, 2). The Tyler concordance (see Selected Bibliography) is a useful companion volume.

4. "Fondement et mode de l'éthique dans les *Fables* de La Fontaine," *Kentucky Romance Quarterly*, 18 (1971), 333–42.

5. "Narrator and Reader: Keys to Irony in La Fontaine," *Australian Journal of French Studies*, 16 (1979), 389–400.

6. Similar issues are likewise the concern of John D. Lyons, "Author and Reader in the *Fables*," *French Review*, 49 (1975), 59–67.

7. *Princeton Encyclopedia of Poetry and Poetics*, ed. Alex Preminger, enlarged edition (Princeton, NJ: Princeton Univ. Press, 1974), p. 12.

8. "Poetic Technique and Meaning in La Fontaine's *Fables*," in *Studies in Romance Languages and Literatures*, ed. Sandra M. Cypess (Lawrence, KS: Coronado Press, 1979), pp. 62–76.

9. *La Fontaine et le premier recueil des "Fables,"* 2 vols. (Paris: Nizet, 1965, 1966).

10. "Signs of Irony in La Fontaine's *Fables*," chapter 6 of her book *Signs of the Hidden: Semiotic Studies* (Amsterdam: Rodopi, 1980), pp. 143–61, is virtually identical—mechanical and minor stylistic changes aside—to an earlier version published in *Papers on French Seventeenth Century Literature*, No. 11 (1979), pp. 51–76; my references have as their source the essay as it appears in *Signs of the Hidden*. See also Jules Brody's incisive analysis of the *PFSCL* version, "Irony in La Fontaine: From Message to Massage," in the same number of that journal, pp. 77–89. No changes in Tiefenbrun's essay are the result of reservations expressed by Brody in his critique.

11. (Paris: Flammarion, 1964).

12. Booth's *A Rhetoric of Irony* and Muecke's *The Compass of Irony* (London: Methuen, 1969) will serve as indispensable touchstones in chapter II; see also Muecke's shorter study, *Irony* (London: Methuen, 1970). The serviceable term ironologist, used by Muecke, will appear in subsequent contexts without quotation marks.

13. "Four Modes of Double Irony in La Fontaine's *Fables*," in *The Equilibrium of Wit: Essays for Odette de Mourgues*, ed. Peter Bayley and Dorothy Gabe Coleman (Lexington, KY: French Forum, Publishers, 1982), pp. 201–12.

14. "La Fontaine's Ironic Vision in the *Fables*," *French Review*, 50 (1977), 562–71.

II

A Theoretical Foundation

The purpose of this chapter is to establish a useful definition of irony in order to be able to talk meaningfully in the remaining chapters about ironic elements in the *Fables*. To proceed in this manner entails a fundamental danger that must be acknowledged at the outset. As E. D. Hirsch, Jr., has warned: "Every interpreter labors under the handicap of an inevitable circularity: all his internal evidence tends to support his hypothesis because much of it was constituted by his hypothesis."[1] In response to such allegations concerning the present study, my only defense would be to say that my point of departure was La Fontaine's poetry rather than any a priori construct. Whereas this chapter will be properly concerned in large measure with insights communicated by ironologists, the central focus of this book is interpretation of literary texts. For many years, close reading of the *Fables* has persuaded me that, at least in a general sense, they are ironic, but this hypothesis cannot progress very far unless it is accompanied by a precise definition of terms. To avoid conveying the impression of having created a convenient "self-confirming hypothesis" (Hirsch), it will be necessary to show that irony (as defined here) can survive the rigorous test of textual analysis. No theoretical underpinning, however logical and comprehensive, can ever save an egregiously wrong-headed reading from an inevitable collapse.

Although irony in various forms has been flourishing since the days of Socrates, Plato, and Aristotle, until our own century it has been (and for some still remains) a

rather nebulous concept: " 'Ironical' without distinguishing qualifications is now in danger of being as uninforma-
tive a term in literary criticism as 'realistic' " (Muecke, *The
Compass of Irony*, p. 13). Fortunately, Muecke has done
criticism a great service by combatting this hazy state of
affairs with remarkable clarity. It should be noted, however, that this lucid ironologist, well aware of the complexities of his subject, does not attempt to provide easy
answers to every imaginable question about irony, for he
acknowledges that he has

> no brief and simple definition that will include all kinds of
> irony while excluding all that is not irony, that distinctions
> from one angle may not be distinctions from another, and
> that kinds of irony theoretically distinguishable will in
> practice be found merging into one another. (p. 14)

At the very least, Muecke supplies a helpful starting point
for anyone desiring to deal with irony in literature on the
level of explication. In discussing his ideas I will make
frequent references to the ironological work of Wayne C.
Booth, whose rhetorical approach to irony is an indispensable complement to Muecke's carefully developed
system of classifications.

"In all instances of irony," Muecke states, "we can distinguish three essential elements" that might be termed
its "formal requirements" as opposed to the "subjective
and aesthetic requirements" of irony (p. 19). Muecke describes the first element as follows:

> In the first place irony is a double-layered or two-storey
> phenomenon. At the lower level is the situation either as
> it appears to the victim of irony (where there is a victim)
> or as it is deceptively presented by the ironist (where
> there is an ironist). . . . At the upper level is the situation
> as it appears to the observer or the ironist. The upper level
> need not be *presented* by the ironist; it need only be evoked
> by him or be present in the mind of the observer. Nor

> need it be more than a hint that the ironist does not quite
> see the situation as he has presented it at the lower level
> ... or that the victim does not see the situation quite as it
> really is. (p. 19)

This two-level figure parallels Booth's image (evoking a notion popular among rhetoricians from antiquity onward) of a "complex dwelling place," except that the process of reconstruction may move in a different (figurative) direction; for Booth, " ... perhaps the implied intellectual motion is really 'downward,' 'going beneath the surface' to something solider or more profound; we rip up a rotten platform and probe to a solid one" (*A Rhetoric of Irony*, pp. 34–35). Choosing between these directional alternatives is not of crucial importance, but both seem to suggest something basic regarding the nature of irony: moving to a higher level in reconstruction implies the vantage-ground shared by ironists and observers (but from which victims of irony are necessarily excluded) while also implying the superior degree of esthetic pleasure to be derived from successfully reconstructing the ironies of a work or passage; moving to a lower level, on the other hand, reflects the architectural principle of tearing down and rebuilding (in a double-layered structure, only the upper level can be demolished if there is to remain a platform on which to stand) and also conveys the idea of digging for hidden elements. Since Muecke does not insist on the presence of either a victim or an ironist, his picture of irony as a "two-storey phenomenon" is flexible enough to accommodate a wide array of ironic structures.

The next element in Muecke's presentation of the essential features of irony is tightly bound to the first:

> In the second place there is always some kind of opposition between the two levels, an opposition that may take the form of contradiction, incongruity, or incompatibility.

> What is said may be contradicted by what is meant . . . ;
> what the victim thinks may be contradicted by what the
> observer knows. . . . It is, however, by no means uncom-
> mon for there to be a further opposition . . . between two
> elements both at the lower level. (pp. 19–20)

To illustrate this kind of lower-level opposition, Muecke
cites an example from *Candide:* the episode in which two
rival kings both celebrate victory as an aftermath of the
same battle. The critic explains:

> . . . there is still an opposition between the upper and
> lower levels, though it may be less apparent; the victory
> that is claimed on the lower level is incompatible with the
> fact that both sides adequately destroyed each other as
> well as the countryside round about. (p. 20)

Evidence of this type of ironic structure leads Muecke to
propose a distinction that will form the basis of David Lee
Rubin's essay on irony in the *Fables:*

> It is, I think, profitable to distinguish "Simple Irony," in
> which the opposition is solely between levels, and "Dou-
> ble Irony" ([William] Empson's term), in which there is
> also a more obvious opposition within the lower level. (p.
> 20)

Citing passages from Flaubert's *Dictionnaire des idées reçues*
and *L'Ile des pingouins* of Anatole France that he views as
analogous to the aforementioned illustration from *Candide,* Muecke describes them as cases in which "the contradiction and mutual destruction directs us to the ironist's real meaning" (p. 24). The cancellation of opposing
viewpoints is likewise a central aspect of Rubin's concern
in his treatment of double irony in the *Fables.*

Whether we are dealing with single or double ironies, it
is important to stress, along with the need for an opposi-

tion in any passage containing irony, Booth's concept of the subtractive nature of irony:

> The metaphor of wax and gold is used by Ethiopians to describe what happens in their ironies: the wax mold melts away, under interpretation, leaving the gold of true meaning—a striking parallel to my account of irony as essentially requiring a negative or "subtractive" step. (*A Rhetoric of Irony*, p. 40, n. 4)

Insistence on the subtractive properties of irony will enable us to distinguish it from the kinds of "prolonged doublings of meaning" found in metaphor, allegory, and fable (apologue), for which we are required "to add meanings, not to see incompatibles and then choose among them" (Booth, p. 24).

The third "formal requirement" of irony, according to Muecke, is "an element of 'innocence'; either a victim is confidently unaware of the very possibility of there being an upper level or point of view that invalidates his own, or an ironist pretends not to be aware of it" (p. 20). The only exception to this principle would be sarcasm or "very overt irony," with which I will not be directly concerned in this study. For Booth, who generally admires Muecke's analysis of irony, the term *innocent* "may be misleading because we must keep in mind how often in irony the 'innocent' is in fact the ironist with whom we choose to dwell, as his innocence undermines the falsely sophisticated . . ." (p. 39), but I think the word will remain serviceable if one remembers that the innocence generated by an ironic structure can be feigned (as a tactic of the ironist) as well as real (from the perspective of the victim). It is important to emphasize the notion of the victim's *confident* unawareness that the apparent could possibly be trumped by the real. In Muecke's view, "All that is necessary is the merest avoidable assumption on the part of the victim that he is not mistaken." As he explains the matter, "Simple ignorance is safe from irony, but ignorance compounded with the least degree of confidence counts as intellectual hubris and is a punishable offence" (p. 30). To be sure, the victim is not alone in being jeopardized by ironic events or situations; as Muecke points out,

> . . . the ironist is equally vulnerable, for the very act of being ironical implies an assumption of superiority, an assumption one cannot make without forgetting either that the tables may be turned . . . or that one may be subject to irony from a level higher than one's own . . . . (p. 31)

The *trompeur trompé* motif is one means by which La Fontaine exploits this chain-reaction potential of irony.

Knowledge of the basic elements of which irony is composed will not provide all the information we need in order to be able to interpret ironic structures in literature. It will be helpful as well to consider some of Muecke's observations concerning the "three grades of irony" (pp. 52–60). The first of these is the overt grade: "In Overt Irony the victim or the reader or both are meant to see the ironist's real meaning at once" (p. 54). La Fontaine's habitual practice of according human speech and customs to animals would appear to be a manifestation of this grade of irony: "What makes irony overt is a blatancy in the ironic contradiction or incongruity" (Muecke, p. 54). No reader is ever going to be fooled by the poetic miracle whereby dogs and wolves and rats express themselves eloquently in French *vers libres*. This technique, in isolation, quickly becomes a cliché: "With every repetition of an ironical expression or device the less effective it becomes as irony" (p. 55). Fortunately, this overt feature of Lafontainian irony does not function solely at a structural—as opposed to textural—level (to preserve Brody's useful distinction); the convention of the verbalizing animal is combined in a typical fable with other ironic features to create works of such richness that close, multiple readings are amply rewarded. Otherwise, of course, far fewer scholars would spend time seriously confronting La Fontaine's complex and varied uses of language.

The second grade of irony, and by far the most fruitful of the three mentioned by Muecke, is the covert grade:

> What distinguishes Covert Irony is that it is intended not to be seen but rather to be detected. The Covert Ironist will aim at avoiding any tone or manner or any stylistic indication that would immediately reveal his irony. The closer he can get to an "innocent" non-ironical way of speaking or writing while at the same time allowing his real meaning to be detected the more subtle his irony. He must, of course, run the risk of having his irony go undetected. (p. 56)

It is most unlikely that all of La Fontaine's covert ironies will ever be detected. The same danger of misinterpretation is faced, as everyone is aware, by any author whose irony is more subtle than the straightforward pronouncement, "How ironic it is that. . ." In handling covert irony, the interpreter must always be careful to ascertain that the material under consideration is really ironic. And it is impossible to be confident that the subject under investigation is irony (rather than something else) without running headlong into the prickly issue of intentionality. In other words, the reader must begin each investigation by assuming that irony in literature is never created by accident. As Muecke declares, "a work can be ironical only by intention," but "an intention to be ironical does not of itself make a work ironical *for the reader*" (pp. 56–57). Since we are unable to interview the historical person Jean de La Fontaine (and even if we could, the discussion, though no doubt fascinating in other respects, might have little if any exegetical value), how are we to attempt to determine his intentions in composing the *Fables?* How can we escape getting trapped in what Wimsatt and Beardsley have called "the intentional fallacy"? Booth points out that these critics "rule out only statements made by the author outside the work about his *motives* or *purposes* or *plans* or *hopes for value*" (p. 126, n. 13). As interpreters we are concerned only with the intentions of Booth's "implied author," who is "part of what the author creates *by* writing the poem." If there is any hope of discovering what the implied author has intended in a literary work, there must be discernible clues in the work itself. It is on this crucial point, I believe, that covert irony differs from the third grade proposed by Muecke, private irony—that is, "irony which is not intended to be perceived either by the victim or anyone else" (p. 59). This type of irony, so arcane as to be for all practical purposes nonexistent, I am satisfied to leave unexplored in the pages to follow. Analyses of private irony are always susceptible to becoming a free-wheeling expression of the critic's private sensibility. Even if someone discovered a letter in which La Fontaine asserted, "My fables are above all an elaborate commentary on French society in the second half of the seventeenth century (I've hidden Fouquet and Colbert everywhere, don't you know?),'' we would have to say that, despite his avowed intention, the irony of these portrayals has generally turned out much too private to be plausibly explicated. If private irony is, then, an exegetical impasse, how can the reader determine whether a work is imbued with covert irony?

The secret, most critics would agree, lies in looking for contextual clues. But knowledge of this essential starting point for critical inquiry is of little help in the abstract. It is no doubt justifiable to contend, with Cleanth Brooks, that any statement found in a poem "bears the pressure of the context and has its meaning modified by the context,''[2] but such awareness will not prove useful until we know exactly what is meant by the term *context*. To talk about the context of a work without defining the word can only produce misunderstandings. It is necessary to bear in mind, as Hirsch notes, that

> . . . a context is something that has itself been determined —first by an author and then, through a construction, by an interpreter. It is not something that is simply there without anybody having to make any determinations. (*Validity in Interpretation,* p. 48)

Hirsch's own view of literary context is very broad, "starting with the words that surround the crux and expanding to the entire physical, psychological, social, and historical milieu in which the utterance occurs," and including as well (among other elements) ". . . the traditions and conventions that the speaker relies on, his attitudes, purposes, kind of vocabulary, relation to his audience . . ." (p. 86). For Hirsch, in the final analysis, "the essential component of a context is the intrinsic genre of the utterance" (p. 87), the "intrinsic genre" being defined as *"that sense of the whole by means of which an interpreter can correctly understand any part in its determinacy"* (p. 86).[3] As for Muecke, his notion of context is equally panoramic:

> What suggests to us that someone is being ironical is, to speak generally, the awareness of a contradiction between what is ostensibly the writer's or speaker's opinion, line of argument, etc., and the whole context within which the opinion or line of argument is presented. The "whole context" comprises *(a)* what we already know (if we know anything) about the writer and the subject, *(b)* what the writer tells us (if he tells us anything) about himself and the subject over and above his pretended meaning, and *(c)* what we are told by the way in which he expresses his opinion, presents his case, or conducts his argument. (p. 58)

Muecke proceeds to reveal numerous ways in which the reader may be able to perceive a contradiction between the ostensible and real sense of an utterance. For example, a historical error may be announced as true (with regard to the *Fables*, which Muecke does not discuss, we readily discern behavioral differences between La Fontaine's animals and their real-world counterparts), or the author's known opinion or character may be contradicted by something in the work. One may also find the writer using, to establish irony, such techniques as "a logical contradiction," "a discordant tone in speaking," or "any discrepancy between what is ostensibly said and the language in which it is expressed . . ." (p. 58). These devices and others will be examined in the course of my discussion of irony in the *Fables*.

The problem of context is likewise an important issue in *A Rhetoric of Irony*. Context, for Booth, is never a conveniently prepackaged commodity.

> Whether a given word or passage or work *is* ironic depends . . . not on the ingenuity of the reader but on the intentions that constitute the creative act. And whether it is *seen* as ironic depends on the reader's catching the proper clues to those intentions. (p. 91)

Although it is the context that provides these clues, as readers we must keep in mind

> that we cannot know in advance which of many possible contextual matters will be relevant—other parts of the work itself, knowledge about the author's life and times, or the reader's deepest convictions about what authors are likely to say in earnest. Even those of us who believe that "the text" is always in some sense final arbiter of meanings will find ourselves using many contexts that according to some critical theories are extrinsic. (p. 91)

Later Booth will assert, in a similar vein, that "a reconstructing of implied authors and implied readers relies on inferences about intentions, and these often depend on our knowing facts from outside the poem'' (p. 133). How can I subscribe to this composite of Muecke, Booth, and Hirsch without committing the fundamental mistake of explaining La Fontaine's poetry on the basis of extraliterary criteria? This apparent dilemma can be solved, I think, if at all times the literary text remains the point of departure for the explicator. Every word in every fable enters the poem equipped with predetermined semantic weight, of course, but only the text can dictate means of evaluating the word's denotative and connotative properties in the closed-circuit environment of the poem. La Fontaine's externally expressed ideas about the functions of literature may offer clues to an understanding of irony in the *Fables*, but such observations must always be justified internally instead of being superimposed from the outside (e.g., the reader is not permitted to apply the fabulist's remark: ''En ces sortes de feinte il faut instruire et plaire, / Et conter pour conter me semble peu d'affaire,'' *F*, VI, 1, willy-nilly to any situation from one end of the *Fables* to the other). Sometimes (especially in chapter V, where I deal with ironic elements in Book X) my context will include works beyond the poem under immediate discussion, but only when the initial context (that of the individual fable as a conceptual unit) clearly lends itself to a broader architectural elaboration.

At this point a brief consideration of Hirsch's viewpoint on meaning, significance, and coherence will be instructive. My inquiry into irony in La Fontaine will be concerned not with significance but with meaning in accordance with the initial distinction proposed here by Hirsch:

Meaning is that which is represented by a text; it is what the author meant by his use of a particular sign sequence; it is what the signs represent. *Significance*, on the other hand, names a relationship between that meaning and a person, or a conception, or a situation, or indeed anything imaginable. (p. 8)

Clearly, significance does not invite strict critical controls because "there is literally no limit to the significance of the shortest and most banal text" (p. 63). The range of literary significance could even include assertions of the type, "How the *Fables* have changed my life" or "What La Fontaine would say about certain wars in the twentieth century." Significance, as Hirsch defines it, need not be a frivolous matter. The critic, having described "understanding" as "a perception or construction of the author's verbal meaning, . . ." adds that "[t]he significance of that meaning, its relation to ourselves, to history, to the author's personality, even to the author's other works can be something equally objective and is frequently even more important" (p. 143). Meaning, however, is a far more manageable, restricted concept: "Verbal meaning is whatever someone has willed to convey by a particular sequence of linguistic signs and which can be conveyed (shared) by means of those linguistic signs" (p. 31). This "provisional" definition is subsequently "expanded and made more descriptive":

> . . . verbal meaning can be defined . . . as a *willed type* which an author expresses by linguistic symbols and which can be understood by another through those symbols. It is essential to emphasize the concept of type since it is only through this concept that verbal meaning can be (as it is) a determinate object of consciousness and yet transcend (as it does) the actual contents of consciousness. (p. 49)

It is undoubtedly true that many of the ironic meanings that I will ascribe to the *Fables* were totally unknown to their author (like the modern terminology that allows me and my contemporaries to discuss literature more specifically than La Fontaine and his contemporaries were able to do), but I will endeavor to demonstrate that such meanings are consistent with what the text informs us the (implied) author intended to convey. To anyone who would react to my analysis by stating, "That's not what La Fontaine meant," I can reply, with Hirsch, "An author almost always means more than he is aware of meaning, since he cannot explicitly pay attention to all the aspects of his meaning" (p. 48). But of course this awareness by itself certainly does not give me license to invent dime-a-dozen meanings that demonstrably run counter to the internal logic of the poetic texts. The key to the testing of hypotheses of meaning is their coherence:

> The self-identity of a verbal meaning depends on a coherence that is at least partly analogous to physical continuity. If a text has traits that point to subconscious meanings (or even conscious ones), these belong to the verbal meaning of the text only if they are coherent with the consciously willed type which defines the meaning as a whole. If such meanings are noncoherent with the willed type, then they do not belong to verbal meaning which is by definition willed. (p. 54)

When I interpret a poem, nothing in my explication should be violated by other contextual elements (however broadly the context in a given instance may be construed). Otherwise my analysis will conflict with the willed meaning. But so long as I respect the principle of coherence, I will be strolling in safe territory. This point will be all the more crucial when my interpretation (as in the case of "Le Loup et le chien") appears in many ways to be irreconcilable with much that informed, intelligent scholars have written about the fable. Nor will I be able to furnish comforting proof of anything (beyond such surface features as syllable counts and rhyme schemes): "The uncertainty of interpretation arises because we can never be absolutely certain that we have premised the right type" (p. 91). In other words, the ironies that I declare attributable to the *Fables* will be potentially amenable to (ironic) reconstruction by critics who are capable of reading La Fontaine with fuller comprehension than I can command. To be sure, if I did not consider my interpretations reasonably cogent I would abandon them, but certainty or proof in such investigations will necessarily be impossible goals. In analyzing the irony of the *Fables* my constant objective will be adherence to what Hirsch calls "validity," which "implies the correspondence of an interpretation to a meaning which is represented by the text . . ." (p. 10). It is important not to forget the rules of this game: "Validity requires a norm—a meaning that is stable and determinate no matter how broad its range of implication and application" (p. 126). The exegetical burden may seem intimidatingly heavy: "A validation has to show not merely that an interpretation is plausible, but that it is the most plausible one available" (p. 171)—a demand that will perhaps prove somewhat easier to meet in some cases than in others. And in the final analysis even the most helpful tenets enunciated by lucid theoreticians will offer limited guidance to the explicator: "The act of understanding is at first a genial (or a mistaken) guess, and there are no methods for making guesses, no rules for generating insights" (p. 203). Nothing could be truer at the level of analysis, but at the preliminary stage—defining basic terms—outside assistance is indispensable. The last planks have not yet been installed in my theoretical foundation. Here I will turn again to Wayne Booth for aid in preventing my quest for irony in the *Fables* from being a series of wild, though well-intentioned, guesses.

Early in *A Rhetoric of Irony,* Booth describes the four steps to be used in reconstructing "stable irony," the type in which, ". . . once a reconstruction of meaning has been made, the reader is not then invited to undermine it with further demolitions and reconstructions" (p. 6). The process by which the reader can decide whether a passage being analyzed really does involve stable irony is explained as follows:

Step one. The reader is required to reject the literal meaning . . . .

Step two. Alternative interpretations or explanations are tried out. . . .

Step three. A decision must . . . be made about the author's knowledge or beliefs. . . . It is this decision about the author's own beliefs that entwines the interpretation of stable ironies so inescapably in intentions. . . . It is true that the author I am interested in is only the creative person responsible for the choices that made the work—what I have elsewhere called the "implied author" who is found in the work itself.

Step four. Having made a decision about the knowledge or beliefs of the speaker, we can finally choose a new meaning or cluster of meanings with which we can rest secure. (pp. 10–12)

This process will strike most people as being firmly rooted in common sense, yet one does not have to look far to find a study of irony that seems crippled precisely because the critic has failed to follow these four simple steps of reconstruction. This does not mean that every time I label a word, passage, or poem of La Fontaine ironic the steps underlying this determination will be paraded across the page. But if at any time the discussion does not spring from these preliminary steps, analytical defects will no doubt be readily apparent.[4]

Before closing this chapter with a consideration of test cases from the *Fables,* I will examine three variables established by Booth in pinpointing types of ironies, aside from nonrhetorical kinds—"that is, all that are not designed by one human being to be shared by at least one other" (p. 234): this category appears to be the one that Muecke calls private irony. As for the others, according to Booth they can be ordered on the basis of "variations in how authors and readers relate" (p. 234). Rhetorical ironies can be (1) overt or covert, (2) stable or unstable, and (3) local or infinite. Booth is careful, however, not to let

himself be carried away by the momentum of these classifications:

> It should be unnecessary at this late date in the twen-
> tieth century, the century of sociology, the century of ma-
> trices, to dwell on the dangers and limitations in talking of
> such types. Those I am distinguishing would be especially
> destructive if they were seen as what authors necessarily
> think of as they write. "I will write a piece of unstable-
> covert-infinite irony." "*Mine* will be unstable-overt-local."
> I am not classifying literary kinds but mutual operations,
> any one of which could be found in a variety of literary
> kinds. (p. 234)

Bearing this caveat in mind, one can find it profitable, in
the arena of practical criticism, to apply Booth's variables.
The first of these (recalling Muecke's first and second
grades) concerns whether the irony is overt or covert:
"*Degree of openness or disguise.* How much secret work
does the author require, if any?" As will be seen, La Fontaine demonstrates ability in manipulating both overt and
covert ironies, though his finest art probably tends
towards the latter, the reader's pleasure being heightened
by the discovery of hidden but discernible invitations to
join the fabulist/narrator in the joyful complicity of ironist
and observer. The second variable involves determining
whether the irony is stable or unstable: "*Degree of stability
in the reconstruction.* How much reason does the reader
have for thinking his immediate task completed once an
asserted irony has been understood or a covert irony has
been reconstructed?" Here the challenge to the critic
becomes more formidable because the process of legitimate reconstruction will depend on deciphering increasingly subtle clues. Booth portrays the two poles of this
variable as separated by a "chasm":

> the fundamental distinction between stable ironies and
> ironies in which the truth asserted or implied is that no

stable reconstruction can be made out of the ruins revealed through the irony. The author—insofar as we can
discover him, and he is often very remote indeed—refuses
to declare himself, however subtly, *for* any stable proposition, even the opposite of whatever proposition his irony
vigorously denies. (p. 240)

It would seem that La Fontaine deals most often with stable ironies, but there are also cases in which he gives evidence of erecting tall hurdles of instability. As for the
third variable, it concerns discovering whether the irony
is local or infinite: *"Scope of the 'truth revealed,'* or ground
covered by the reconstruction or assertion, ranging from
local through grand-but-still-finite to 'absolute infinite
negativity.' How far is the reader asked to travel on the
road to complete negation, and how does he know when
to stop?" (p. 234). Ironies of the first type are judged to be
"finite in application" because their "reconstructed meanings are in some sense local, limited" (p. 6): for instance,
the irony of a poem by La Fontaine would be termed local
if its intent involved a single realm of human activity; in
"L'Avare qui a perdu son trésor" (*F*, IV, 20), when the
poet says that the miser "Ne possédait pas l'or, mais l'or
le possédait," at first glance the second hemistich appears
to be an exact reversal of the first, but in fact the kind of
possession described by the utterance "l'or le possédait"
has many connotations—the needless forfeiting of life's
possibilities, the virtual bondage of the man controlled by
his wealth, and so on—that are absent from the simple
notion of a human being possessing gold; yet the reader is
not free to search for infinitely added levels of applicability
because the irony allows itself to be contained by the initial
reconstruction. Infinite ironies, on the other hand, are apparently the product of a more pervasively cynical age than
La Fontaine's. If one accepts Booth's distinction between
works like Howard Nemerov's poem "Boom!" and works
displaying infinite ironies (e.g., "Black Rook in Rainy

Weather" by Sylvia Plath, "Warning to Children" by Robert Graves, and Samuel Beckett's novel *The Unnamable),* it seems unlikely that any of La Fontaine's ironies roam beyond the terrain of local, finite excavations:

> The borderline between a poem like "Boom!" and works that assert infinite ironies may be dim, but there is nevertheless a real difference between the still quite local underminings in the one and the unqualified cosmic assertion that the universe—not just this or that effort of man to grasp it—is absurd: no truth, no passion, no political commitment, no moral judgment, will stand up under ironic examination. (p. 253)

Thus, although the degree of openness and of stability may vary in the ironies that inhabit the *Fables,* the ultimate boundaries of reconstruction are functional and adequately marked. This does not suggest, however, that in reading La Fontaine's ironies the critic necessarily strives for the deceptive warmth of unambiguous meanings (unfortunately a natural tendency when one confronts a genre with aphoristic roots). Hirsch's remarks on determinacy and imprecision are apposite:

> Determinacy is a necessary attribute of any sharable meaning, since an indeterminacy cannot be shared: if a meaning were indeterminate, it would have no boundaries, no self-identity, and therefore could have no identity with a meaning entertained by someone else. But determinacy does not mean definiteness or precision. Undoubtedly, most verbal meanings are imprecise and ambiguous, and to call them such is to acknowledge their determinacy: they are what they are—namely ambiguous and imprecise—and they are not univocal and precise. (p. 44)

In each act of reconstruction, the context—properly surveyed—should inform the critic whether a search for multivalence is warranted. Nothing can be accomplished by inventing ambiguities where none exist, but a common problem in interpretation of the *Fables* has been to ignore contextual clues and thus to stop short of full (and often ambiguous) reconstruction of meanings. In other words, La Fontaine's esthetically appropriate verbal craftiness has frequently been underestimated, with a net loss to appreciation of his art—the quicksand art of a master ironist.

The only theoretical element remaining to be discussed is that of the observer's attitude toward ironic situations and events. As Booth's rhetorical approach makes clear, a corollary of Muecke's "confident unawareness" principle (that someone must either be or seem to be fooled by words or circumstances) is that the reader or spectator must be enlightened, capable of distinguishing what is contextually real from what, in the work, is illusory. Irony, in literature as in life, cannot exist in a vacuum. Devoid of a frame of reference, irony ceases to be ironic. This we know. But it might also be worthwhile, before proceeding, to consider the emotions that irony is likely to produce in the observer. For the reader of the *Fables* these tend to be comic responses, though reactions may be quite complex. The need for yet another definition immediately arises, but the following distinction, proposed by Elder Olson, will perhaps allow us to sail clear of semantic reefs:

> We may take a grave or a lighthearted view of human life and actions; tragedy develops out of the grave view as comedy does out of the lighthearted. . . . It is not the events by themselves which are matter for gravity or levity; it is the view taken of them. . . . When we say . . . that tragedy imitates a serious action, we mean that it imitates an action *which it makes serious;* and comparably, comedy imitates an action *which it makes a matter for levity.*[5]

When analyzing this factor (whatever the observer's response to a word, passage, or work), we run the risk of getting lost in the dark and dangerous forests of "affective fallacy." Yet if we isolate the causes of irony from its effects, how can we be sure that the texts we have chosen to label ironic are in fact that? When dealing with irony or any other literary problem, there is no way—and certainly no reason—to escape the recipient (that is, the observer, spectator, or reader).

A. R. Thompson has used the phrase "painfully comic" to characterize an aspect of three types of ironic expression: "irony of speech (verbal irony)," "irony of character (irony of manner)," and "irony of events (dramatic irony)."[6] Putting aside the matter of the range of potential reactions to irony throughout literature, I would say that the adverb *painfully* is an inappropriate descriptor of typical responses to irony in the *Fables*. In this poetry, what Cleanth Brooks calls "the pressure of the context" (however defined, but especially the immediate poetic environment) often combats potentially painful reactions.[7] This is not the occasion to explore the intriguing implications of Jacques Gaucheron's contention that "toute l'oeuvre de La Fontaine est le refus d'un univers tragique,"[8] but he is unquestionably closer to the truth—at least insofar as the *Fables* are concerned—than those who insist on attributing to the fabulist a general seriousness of purpose beyond the commitment to art that the very existence of these poems implies. Abstracted from their context, many of the fables would be capable of evoking "painfully comic" reactions. But La Fontaine skillfully undermines feelings of pain or empathy that might be aroused. "Les Obsèques de la lionne" (VIII, 14) is a fable that illustrates the point well. Here, as elsewhere throughout the *Fables*, the use of nonhuman personages functions as a distancing mechanism, guaranteeing the reader's emotional detachment while at the same time suggesting, through various personifying devices, that people and animals may not differ very much after all in certain fundamental respects. No matter how much they may resemble us, however, the plight of La Fontaine's nonhuman characters will never move us as deeply as Andromaque's dilemma or the misfortunes of Hippolyte; but this does not mean that we must read the *Fables* from a standpoint of anthropocentric superiority, because such a stance would frequently be undercut from the outset. At any rate, in "Les Obsèques de la lionne" the poet creates a tone that prevents us from empathizing with the grief-stricken lion: he does this, for instance, by using inversion and by rhyming paired octosyllabic lines ("Le Prince aux cris s'abandonna, / Et tout son antre en résonna"); by employing language that would ring false in an elegiac poem (the courtiers are called "Peuple caméléon, peuple singe du maître"); by parodying noble discourse when the lion addresses the stag who has with good reason refused to mourn ("Nous n'appliquerons point sur tes membres profanes / Nos sacrés ongles"); and of course by reinforcing the ironic intersection of human and animal planes ("Prince," "Province," "Prévôts," "Reine," "Roi," "Champs Elysiens").

Even when La Fontaine's characters are human beings, the fabulist does not normally permit us to become involved in their plight. In "Le Trésor et les deux hommes" (IX, 16), we are first introduced to a man without money—"logeant le Diable en sa bourse"—who decides in despair to hang himself. The narrator notes lightly that in any event the man would die of hunger: "Genre de mort qui ne duit pas / A gens peu curieux de goûter le trépas." As it happens, however, the wall to which the man has attached his suicide rope "S'ébranle aux premiers coups, tombe avec un trésor." No longer having a motive for killing himself, the man goes away with his fortune. The rope does not long remain idle, however, because the first man has inevitably become wealthy at another's expense: "L'homme au trésor arrive, et trouve son argent / Absent."

This amusingly compressed rhyme prepares us to view the hanging scene as a comical event, as a ritual enacted in a distant, Chaplinesque universe: "Le lacs était tout prêt; il n'y manquait qu'un homme: / Celui-ci se l'attache, et se pend bien et beau." As the narrator implies in an understated formula, the episode has resulted in the restoration of order: "Aussi bien que l'argent le licou trouva maître." As these typical examples reveal, Thompson's phrase "painfully comic" does not adequately describe the effect of ironic devices in the *Fables,* though this obviously does not rule out the possible pertinence of the adverb in other ironic situations.

On the other hand, it is important to retain the second term, *comic,* when studying reactions to irony in the *Fables.* Why is it that an ironic structure in literature is likely to produce a response containing a comic ingredient? Part of the answer undoubtedly lies in the probable position of the reader or spectator relative to the victim or target of irony. As Northrop Frye has theorized, "if inferior in power or intelligence to ourselves, so that we have the sense of looking down on a scene of bondage, frustration or absurdity, the hero belongs to the *ironic* mode."[9] The hypothetical mode being posited here might well include a large number of nonironic structures as well as ironic ones, but it is true that La Fontaine employs many techniques to ensure that the reader will be able to observe the fable characters from a position of superiority. The figurative height of the observation point suggests another aspect of the reader's likely (though not inevitable) reaction: detachment. This may seem to entail an over-subtle distinction without a difference. But detachment is not a necessary attribute of superiority. An illustration from recent French theater will perhaps make this clear. When we read or watch *En attendant Godot,* we have many opportunities to feel superior first to Estragon and Vladimir, then to Pozzo and Lucky: we are capable of reasoning more clearly than they do, and we readily perceive inconsistencies between their words and deeds. And yet the situation of these clown-like individuals finally seems so similar to that of struggling, striving nuclear-age humanity that a typical reaction to the events unfolding in *Godot* might be close to what Thompson terms the "painfully comic" effect of irony, or perhaps even closer to Marcel Gutwirth's unforgettable phrase concerning the psychological basis of laughter: *"Le rire . . . est la conscience joyeuse de notre finitude."*[10] It might therefore be postulated that the intensity of the painful response will vary inversely with the observer's detachment, whereas the intensity of the comic response varies directly with the observer's degree of detachment from the ironic written work or performance. That is, the reader or spectator who is emotionally and intellectually removed from an ironic situation—as is generally the case in the *Fables* of La Fontaine—will above all think it is funny; as the observer's emotional and intellectual distance from the ironic situation is reduced (as in the story of Oedipus), his comic response, although never completely effaced, will be tempered by more sober—or more painful —sentiments. (In the context of the Oedipus legend, the term *comic* would undoubtedly assume a broad meaning to describe our delight that we are more perceptive than the King of Thebes.)

I shall now conclude this chapter by discussing two poems that illustrate how irony, as defined by leading ironologists whose theories have been highlighted above, operates in the *Fables*. I have selected these poems as a bridge from theory to application because they are to an extent thematically related and because they display numerous ironic techniques. Both feature human personages, but irony in the *Fables* is prevalent among all kinds of characters—those representing humans, animals, pots, plants, and deities. Indeed, irony leaves distinguishing marks on virtually every fable in the twelve books.

Some talents of La Fontaine the ironist are effectively

displayed in "Le Curé et le mort" (VII, 10). Even when abstracted from the context of the full poem, the basic event of the fable is clearly ironic: a priest in a funeral cortege dies when his parishioner's coffin, striking him, fractures his skull. On this level, the appearance is the expectation that the episode will take place in the customary manner—with the living burying the dead; in conflict with this normal procedure is the surprising reality of the dénouement. It would be possible for an author to present this unfortunate reversal in a tragic or otherwise somber light. La Fontaine develops the situation in such a way, however, that its inherently ironic properties are intensified.

The poem's ironic environment is created at the very start. Consider the first four lines:

> Un mort s'en allait tristement
> S'emparer de son dernier gîte;
> Un Curé s'en allait gaiement
> Enterrer ce mort au plus vite.

The two characters are contrasted by way of parallel structures. Their ostensible similarity is underlined by rhyme and rhythm: each personage is introduced in two octosyllabic lines; the syntactic structure of line one is repeated in line three; the superficial relationship between the priest and the dead man is emphasized by the *abab* rhyming pattern. But this formal resemblance is contradicted by the situation. The sadness of the dead man is opposed to the priest's gaiety. Both adverbs, *tristement* and *gaiement*, are being used ironically. The first obviously does not mean what it says. On the basis of what we know about corpses, we may assume that this one is not really sad, but rather that the narrator is imputing to the dead body an emotion that in the circumstances would seem appropriate. The priest's happiness is ironic for a different reason. His attitude is in conflict with what the reader holds to be the norm for behavior at a funeral, yet the character appears unaware of this gap; already the reader is invited to put himself in a superior ethical position with respect to the *curé*. It was surprising to learn of the dead man's alleged sadness, and it is likewise counter to our expectation that he should "s'emparer de son dernier gîte"; it is unusual to apply so vigorously active a verb as *s'emparer* to something that is or has become inanimate, and the tone of the line is in tension with the topic. The anecdote is being related without pathos or pity. The semantic opposition of *tristement / gaiement* is elaborated by the rhyming pair of lines two and four (*gîte* and *vite*), where the permanent repose of the deceased is contrasted with the rapid movement of the priest, whose plan—"Enterrer ce mort au plus vite"—is again contrary to what one might call (at the risk, perhaps, of question-begging) the reader's norm. In short, the first four lines of "Le Curé et le mort" provide a foundation for the poem's ironic strategy. We are prepared to view the priest as the victim of irony that he will finally turn out to be. His departure from conventional conduct serves two functions: it prompts us to judge him inferior to ourselves and it allows us to approach the poem with the expectation that emotions usually associated with burial (such as sorrow, regret, loneliness, fear of the future) will all be out of season here. The violent effect of the climactic incident that interrupts the priest's pleasant reverie (concerning how he will spend his funeral fees) is undermined by a barrage of ironic devices:

> Un heurt survient, adieu le char.
> Voilà Messire Jean Chouart
> Qui du choc de son mort a la tête cassée:
> Le Paroissien en plomb entraîne son Pasteur;
> Notre Curé suit son Seigneur;
> Tous deux s'en vont de compagnie.

The reference to "Messire Jean Chouart" would have been recognized by La Fontaine's literate contemporaries as an allusion to Rabelais, who gave the name a phallic implication.[11] In recreative as well as in procreative terms, the priest is officially the antithesis of a Chouart, an opposition that is further underlined by the idea of death permanently ending anyone's fertility. Another ironic element in this passage is the insistent use of possessives. As Margaret Guiton has noted in reference to several fables (including this one), "events always conspire to destroy the validity of the spurious possessive pronoun"— or adjective.[12] Earlier in the poem the priest "couvait des yeux son mort" who symbolized for him, with the emphasis of comic rhymed association, "ce trésor." Now, with the fatal "choc de son mort," the priest finds the sense of *son* subtracted from the repeated possessive expression. In the memorable alexandrine, "Le Paroissien en plomb entraîne son Pasteur," the man ostensibly possessed becomes possessor and unexpectedly triumphant in a reversal all the more striking because, as Couton points out, citing the dictionary of Furetière (*F*, p. 474, n. 5), the phrase "en plomb" underscores the fact that the "Paroissien" is dead. The character who had seemingly controlled the pace of the burial ceremony now "suit son Seigneur," and this possessive establishes a new hierarchical relationship between the two personages, a ranking aurally punctuated by the rhyming of "son Pasteur" with "son Seigneur." The one who would lead has himself been led; the apparent master of the situation has been mastered. The ultimate possessors turn out to be the fabulist/narrator and his mute but mentally active accomplice-in-irony, the reader: early in the poem the dead man had been called "Notre défunt," and now "Notre Curé" belongs as well to the ironist and his *compagnon de lecture*.

"La Jeune Veuve" (VI, 21) is an earlier fable (the final one in the 1668 collection except for the "Epilogue") illustrating other techniques of La Fontaine the ironist. The first fifteen lines of this poem involve the use of dramatic irony, a term initially referring, of course, to a situation in which a character knows less than the audience and possibly less than one or more other characters on stage. Dramatic irony, in the theater and elsewhere, focuses on distinctions between appearance and reality, emphasizes the victim's unawareness of this distinction, and flatters the enlightened observer's feeling of superiority and possibly of detachment. The subject of "La Jeune Veuve" might be stated in platitudinous form: time conquers grief, a theme capable of being developed in various tonalities. La Fontaine opts for irony. At the outset, even before the young mourner is introduced, the poet provides a broad ironic perspective from which we, like spectators at a theatrical performance who are better informed than one or more of the characters, shall be able to react to her initial emotions:

> La perte d'un époux ne va point sans soupirs.
> On fait beaucoup de bruit, et puis on se console.
> Sur les ailes du Temps la tristesse s'envole;
> Le Temps ramène les plaisirs.

Already the reader is being distanced from the episode soon to be presented. Just as words tend to assume a humorous quality when they rhyme very richly, so excessive alliteration, as in line one of this poem (*perte, époux, point, soupirs*), a series of pounding plosives, can serve to lighten the effect of the idea being expressed (the initial consonants of *Paroissien, plomb,* and *Pasteur* in "Le Curé et le mort" function in the same way). The widow's grief is mocked in advance, for the narrator describes audible mourning as a lot of noise, thereby reducing the activity to the common denominator it shares with the barking of an angry dog or the clattering of kitchen utensils. In addition, the narrator cleverly discounts the significance of grief by compressing into a single alexandrine the whole process of mourning and recovery ("On fait beaucoup de bruit, et puis on se console"). In the third line, rhythm and thought conspire to undercut the customary import of grief: the imaginary flight of sadness on Time's wings is conveyed with anapestic swiftness ("Sur les ailes du Temps la tristesse s'envole"). And before long, pleasures return to fill this void ("Le Temps ramène les plaisirs").

The next eleven lines develop this theme of the transformations brought about by the passage of time. In "Le Curé et le mort," the poet employs parallel structures, as we have seen, to contrast two unlike individuals. Here he uses a simpler form of the same device: "Entre la Veuve d'une année / Et la Veuve d'une journée / La différence est grande." In this poem the same person (a widow) is viewed in successive time periods; the fabulist will demonstrate that the apparent resemblance between "la veuve d'une année" and "la veuve d'une journée" is based on sound rather than sense. By the time we reach the end of the fifteen-line introduction (constituting nearly one third of the total poem), we are prepared to react to the young woman's plight from an ironic vantage point, given our superior knowledge of the dynamics of grief (in this poem's frame of reference). Here La Fontaine has recourse to overt, stable, local irony, which does not suffer a loss in amusement value though it is perhaps a more primitive or elementary type of irony than some others to be examined in this study.

We learn that the husband of the attractive young title character has died (La Fontaine maintains the witty tone of the opening lines by resorting to the periphrasis "Partait pour l'autre monde"). Since we correctly predict that time will heal the widow's sorrow, we find her outcry excessive ('Attends-moi, je te suis; et mon âme, / Aussi bien que la tienne, est prête à s'envoler"), an outpouring of emotion that in another context (a Racinian tragedy, for instance, or a story of real-life deprivation) might be judged proper and moving. The poet reintroduces the verb *s'envo-*

ler, used earlier to describe the voyage of sadness transported by time; in the second case, however, *s'envoler* refers to a journey that we surmise will not take place. Indeed it does not, as the fabulist suggests in a crisp
octosyllable: "Le Mari fait seul le voyage." By calling
death "le voyage" and by depriving it of descriptive ad-
jectives (such as *lugubre, morne, triste, fatal*) that would
add emotional weight to the expression, La Fontaine preserves the ironic distance needed to keep the subject far
away from the realm of sentimentality.

Next the poet presents the widow's father, "homme
prudent et sage," who appears to share the reader's
awareness that mourners do not cry forever. He first
reacts to his daughter's anguish by simply letting her
tears flow ("Il laissa le torrent couler"). Subsequently he
does not encourage her to continue, his first spoken
words showing not a trace of tenderness or empathy
("Ma fille, lui dit-il, c'est trop verser de larmes"). How,
he wonders, will the dead man profit if his widow
drowns her charms? Life, in the father's hedonistic opinion, is meant to be lived ("Puisqu'il est des vivants, ne
songez plus aux morts"). Without expecting his daughter
to consent immediately to another wedding, he dares to
mention an indefinite future time when she would do
well to consider remarrying ("souffrez qu'on vous propose / Un époux bien fait, jeune, et tout autre chose / Que
le défunt"). But the daughter is in no mood to listen to talk
of wedding bells; in an overdramatic pronouncement
worthy of an Hugolian protagonist she declares, "Un Cloî-
tre est l'époux qu'il me faut." This expression contributes
to the irony of the poem and further separates the reader
from the widow; the former quickly recognizes as absurd
the idea that a convent might literally, physically, replace
the widow's husband, whatever else a cloistered life might
provide. At the same time, this mention of a convent marks
a change in the widow's emotional state: she is no longer
asking to join her spouse in death. Her father permits the

young woman to go on mourning ("Le père lui laissa digérer sa disgrâce"). The concrete meaning of *digérer* makes
the expression even funnier—and more out of tune with a
respectful consideration of grief—than the figurative
phrase considered by itself.

As time passes in the poem, there are adjustments in
the life of this widow who had wanted to die or to retreat
into a convent. The first alterations are exterior: each day
something is changed "à l'habit, au linge, à la coiffure."
As a matter of fact, mourning proves in one sense to be
advantageous ("Le deuil enfin sert de parure, / En attendant d'autres atours"). There are also changes in the
widow's mental state and behavior:

> Toute la bande des Amours
> Revient au colombier: les jeux, les ris, la danse,
> Ont aussi leur tour à la fin.

In his first-rate study of style in the *Fables,* Jean Dominique Biard states that the initial images of the above passage "are particularly well-chosen since mythology has
endowed the *Amours* with wings."[13] Though conventional, the image of concretized emotions ("Toute la bande
des Amours") returning like a flock of birds to their
dwelling place is very effective here as it contrasts sharply
with the widow's first response to loss and recalls the
lilting phrase in line three, "Sur les ailes du Temps la
tristesse s'envole." The young woman who could previously think only of dying or of being wedded to a cloister
now seems preoccupied by efforts to preserve her youth
or to restore it from the ravages wrought by grief: "On se
plonge soir et matin / Dans la fontaine de Jouvence" (the
legendary source of rejuvenation). And her father? These
transformations have by no means displeased him: "Le
Père ne craint plus ce défunt tant chéri." We are reminded
that the postulate pronounced early in the poem—that a
mourner's noisemaking is followed by consolation—will

also in this instance be fulfilled. The deceased person, sardonically called "ce défunt tant chéri," is by implication viewed here as an adversary, an opponent no longer to be feared. He is quite literally *defunctus*, having completed not only his life but also the influence it might have exercised through memory.[14] The father says nothing more to "notre belle." No persuasion is necessary. This is made obvious by the question that the widow addresses to her father at the end of the poem: "Où donc est le jeune mari / Que vous m'avez promis? dit-elle." The transformation is complete. The pleasure we have experienced in watching the widow change from a *veuve douloureuse* into a *veuve joyeuse* is largely attributable to the poet's finesse in constructing the fable in an ironic mode. The fabulist has successfully developed a dichotomy of appearance and reality, emphasizing the widow's unawareness—perceived from the outset by the reader—that what seems to be real differs from what, in the poem's context, is real. He has ordered the raw materials of the narrative in such a way as to invite a response reflecting the observer's view that the ironic situation is essentially comic, for, unlike the young woman in the poem, we are aware of the salutary effect that the passage of time will have (at least in these circumstances). Thus we find ourselves, as Frye says, "looking down on a scene of bondage, frustration or absurdity." The tone of "La Jeune Veuve" and "Le Curé et le mort" brings to mind the observation of Jankélévitch that "ironiser sur le tragique destinal, c'est . . . affecter de le traiter comme on traite les anecdotes et faits divers de la semaine" (*L'Ironie*, p. 155). In these poems La Fontaine's ironically ordered ". . . comic action . . . neutralizes the emotions of pity and fear to produce the *contrary* . . . of the serious" (Olson, *The Theory of Comedy*, p. 37; he does not apply this principle to the *Fables*).

But our fabulist proved himself to be the tireless inventor of many kinds of irony. How is it possible to reconcile his generally comic outlook with the apologue's moral heritage, which to some extent La Fontaine has evidently preserved? Part of the solution can surely be discovered if one explores connections between irony and closure. This fascinating topic will form the substance of the next chapter.

NOTES

1. *Validity in Interpretation* (New Haven: Yale Univ. Press, 1967), p. 166.
2. "Irony as a Principle of Structure," in *Literary Opinion in America*, ed. Morton Zabel, 3rd ed. (New York: Harper & Row, 1962), p. 731.
3. I hope my treatment in this chapter of such brilliant theoreticians as Hirsch, Booth, and Muecke appears in no way cavalier. Although I am being careful not to distort their ideas, isolated quotations used to clarify my own immediate preoccupations cannot possibly do justice to the scope of their presentations. If any readers find my citations too fragmentary or somehow unclear, I can only advise that they peruse—and savor—*Validity in Interpretation, A Rhetoric of Irony,* and *The Compass of Irony.*
4. For a greatly expanded consideration of the problem of determining whether a text contains clues to irony, see Booth's third chapter, "Is It Ironic?" (pp. 47–86).
5. *The Theory of Comedy* (Bloomington: Indiana Univ. Press, 1968), pp. 35–36. I do not claim that the sentences quoted here do justice to the nuances of Olson's argument, but the notion of literary manner controlling all subject matter is, even in isolation, an essential concept with great relevance for the explicator of La Fontaine.
6. Allan Reynolds Thompson, *The Dry Mock: A Study of Irony in Drama* (Berkeley: Univ. of California Press, 1948), pp. 5, 7, 9.
7. Similarly, in his study *Molière as Ironic Contemplator,* Alvin Eustis has objected to Thompson's view that "irony evokes painful associations in the spectator" because he does not

believe the formula accurately describes the functioning of ironic devices in Molière's plays and in preromantic theater in general (The Hague: Mouton, 1973), p. 13.

8. "Jean de La Fontaine," *Europe*, No. 426 (Oct. 1964), p. 118.

9. *Anatomy of Criticism: Four Essays* (Princeton: Princeton Univ. Press, 1957), p. 34.

10. *Molière ou l'invention comique: La Métamorphose des thèmes et la création des types* (Paris: Minard, 1966), p. 10.

11. See Couton's remarks in *F*, pp. 473–74, n. 3; see also *Fables, contes et nouvelles*, ed. René Groos and Jacques Schiffrin, Vol. 1 of *La Fontaine: Oeuvres complètes*, Bibliothèque de la Pléiade (Paris: Gallimard, 1954), p. 734, n. 4.

12. *La Fontaine: Poet and Counterpoet* (New Brunswick, NJ: Rutgers Univ. Press, 1961), p. 106.

13. *The Style of La Fontaine's Fables* (New York: Barnes & Noble, 1966), p. 180.

14. This Latin term is the past participle of *defungi*, meaning "accomplir sa vie": Albert Dauzat, Jean Dubois, and Henri Mitterand, *Nouveau Dictionnaire étymologique et historique* (Paris: Larousse, 1964), p. 225. Subsequent references to this work will be abbreviated *NDE* and parenthesized in my text.

III

Irony and Closure

La Fontaine's irony in the *Fables*, constantly imbued with comic resonances, need not be considered irreconcilable with the moral philosophy that has often been ascribed to this poetry. Perhaps it is less a matter of incompatibility than of choosing the proper balance when emphasizing these elements. To determine the ultimate meaning of the *Fables* (in the sense proposed by Hirsch), irony appears to be the most promising avenue of inquiry, whereas the philosophical dimension seems to be one of countless possible levels of significance. I do not fundamentally disagree with Emile Baudin's thesis that the philosophy of the *Fables* "est un pur eudémonisme, un pur utilitarisme" constituting a virtual catalogue of Epicurean themes (though at times he too readily assumes the reader's familiarity with precise Epicurean analogues).[1] On the other hand, I believe that Simone Blavier-Paquot overstates the case when she declares that ". . . l'intention gnomique est, chez La Fontaine, . . . le caractère le plus général, le caractère essentiel de la fable" or that ". . . le souci de mener le lecteur à une instruction apparaît dans presque toutes les fables. . . ."[2] Blavier-Paquot is by no means restrictive in her consideration of this element. In her view, the designation of *moraliste* can have relatively wide-ranging applications, referring to

> . . . l'écrivain traitant des moeurs, qu'il formule des réflexions sur les actes, sur le caractère des hommes, ou qu'il peigne la nature humaine, ses vices, ses ridicules, ou encore qu'il disserte sur la loi morale et la règle de nos activités. . . . (p. 21)

And she is aware that the activity of the moralist should be analyzed in light of the overall preoccupations of the poet:

> Outre qu'il fait plus souvent oeuvre de psychologue et de peintre que de moralisateur, La Fontaine, comme moraliste, doit une part de sa réussite à son talent de poète. On ne saurait traiter de l'un en négligeant l'autre. (p. 21)

But the primacy accorded to "l'intention gnomique" reflects a tendency to favor what the poetry says at the expense of what it is and what it does. If La Fontaine had wanted to be a pulpiteer, it is logical to suppose that he would have chosen a more suitable predicatory forum than finely crafted *vers libres.* Statement is part of the package, but as Renée Kohn has noted, La Fontaine in the *Fables* "n'est pas créateur de proverbes."[3] She adds:

> Un proverbe, sous sa plume, perd de son pouvoir d'inertie, de sa lourdeur, cesse de n'être que l'expression du bon sens pratique, se prête à diverses interprétations, devient devise, énigme, pose un problème. . . . (p. 144)

If, as Kohn contends, the *Fables* "apparaissent comme formant un tout . . . ," it follows that "le détail ne prend sa vraie valeur que situé à son exacte place dans l'ensemble" (p. 145). My central concern in this chapter will be to place the *détail* of moral statement or implication, in selected poems, in a fuller (ironic) setting.

Although in historical terms (with antiquity as the starting point) the fable might be described as "essentiellement un petit récit allégorique à l'intention moralisatrice,"[4] when La Fontaine decided to compose fables he had in mind a much broader—and more literary—definition of the traditionally didactic genre. Recognizing that his readers were certain to be acquainted with the basic themes developed in his fables, he remarked, "je ne ferais rien si je ne les rendais nouvelles par quelques traits qui en relevassent le goût" (preface to the 1668 collection: *F*, p. 7). He was well aware that the literary taste of the enlightened public of his age required more than flat, unoriginal moralizing ("C'est ce qu'on demande aujourd'hui: on veut de la nouveauté et de la gaieté," p. 7). Therefore, while downplaying the fable's tendency to sermonize, he wanted to create more enjoyable works: "Je n'appelle pas gaieté ce qui excite le rire; mais un certain charme, un air agréable qu'on peut donner à toutes sortes de sujets, même les plus sérieux" (pp. 7–8). He did, however, acknowledge both parts of the famous dictum of the Roman poet Horace: to mix *utile dulci* (the useful with the agreeable). The instructional dimension had been central before his time, and he did not forget the tradition from which his poetry sprang. Addressing the Dauphin in a short poem introducing the 1668 collection, he declares: "Je me sers d'Animaux pour instruire les Hommes" (*F*, p. 31). He aspires to impart a lesson in his fables as the Aesopic apologues had done:

> Quant au principal but qu'Esope se propose,
>   J'y tombe au moins mal que je puis.
> Enfin si dans ces Vers je ne plais et n'instruis,
> Il ne tient pas à moi, c'est toujours quelque chose.
> (V, 1)

In another poem in the same collection the fabulist explains why he considers it necessary to combine the useful with the agreeable:

> Une Morale nue apporte de l'ennui;
> Le conte fait passer le précepte avec lui.
> En ces sortes de feinte il faut instruire et plaire,
> Et conter pour conter me semble peu d'affaire. (VI, 1)

His attitude toward compositional rules for the tale is different, however; he states that ". . . ce n'est ni le vrai ni le vraisemblable qui font la beauté et la grâce de ces choses-ci; c'est seulement la manière de les conter" (preface to the first volume of *Contes: C*, p. 5). Whatever the genre, La Fontaine, like other members of his literary generation, aims to please: "On ne considère en France que ce qui plaît: c'est la grande règle, et pour ainsi dire la seule" (preface to 1668 *Fables: F*, p. 10). In the preface to his novel *Psyché*, La Fontaine echoes this notion: "Mon principal but est toujours de plaire: pour en venir là, je considère le goût du siècle" (*OD*, p. 123). He intended both to teach and to please his readers, but in practice the former element is consistently subordinated to the latter. Henri Peyre has aptly described the French writers of La Fontaine's period in these terms: "Nos classiques sont des psychologues et des artistes avant tout, des moralistes parfois, mais seulement par surcroît."[5] How can it be shown that *dulce* is more important than *utile* as a factor contributing to La Fontaine's exceptional talent as a fabulist? The challenge of demonstrating this proposition can be partly met if one focuses on the delicate problem of closure in the *Fables:* how the poems conclude.

In her excellent book about closure in poetry, Barbara Herrnstein Smith (who does not, incidentally, discuss any works of La Fontaine) offers this workable basic definition of the concept:

> Closure occurs when the concluding portion of a poem creates in the reader a sense of appropriate cessation. It announces and justifies the absence of further development; it reinforces the feeling of finality, completion, and composure which we value in all works of art; and it gives ultimate unity and coherence to the reader's experience of the poem by providing a point from which all the preceding elements may be viewed comprehensively and their relations grasped as part of a significant design.[6]

It is essential to keep in mind that the properly closed poem does not merely stop. It ends only when completed. La Fontaine uses a wide array of techniques in order to achieve, poem by poem, esthetically satisfying conclusiveness. Never does the moral by itself perform this demanding service, and sometimes it even thwarts effective closure.

Whatever its potential strengths and liabilities, the summarizing aphorism did sometimes prove irresistible to the fabulist. For instance, he ends "Le Renard et le bouc" (III, 5) with the authoritative alexandrine: "En toute chose il faut considérer la fin." This notion applies perfectly to the poem's victim of irony, a billy-goat who, figuratively, "ne voyait pas plus loin que son nez" and who as a consequence found himself stranded at the bottom of a well. Closural effect is obtained here by "formal structure" as well as by "thematic structure" (Smith's terms). The sense of finality is heightened in this case by "the terminal modification of a formal principle" (Smith, p. 92): the concluding rhymed couplet (*fin* echoing *chemin*) differs from the rhyming pattern of the immediately preceding lines. And the very mention of *fin* may have closural relevance: "Allusions to any of the 'natural' stopping places of our lives and experiences—sleep, death, winter, and so forth—tend to give closural force when they appear as terminal features in a poem . . ." (Smith, p. 102). To be sure, the typographical arrangement of each fable can become a factor in the reader's perception of conclusiveness (". . . we tend to impose closure on what is known, independently, to be the terminal point of a sequence": Smith, p. 41), but such visual reinforcement will not suffice in the absence of other, artistically more sophisticated, closural clues.

In "La Montagne qui accouche" (V, 10), the mountain whose offspring is merely a mouse is compared with a vain writer who may promise more than he can deliver

("Je chanterai la guerre / Que firent les Titans au Maître du tonnerre"):

> C'est promettre beaucoup: mais qu'en sort-il souvent?
> Du vent.

The *rime en écho* completed in the bisyllabic last line reinforces the irony of vainly vaunted expectations, recalling the deflationary rhyme of *Paris* with *Souris* given earlier in the poem (it was widely thought that the mountain "... accoucherait, sans faute, / D'une Cité plus grosse que Paris: / Elle accoucha d'une Souris"). The use of a two-syllable line at the end of a poem that had previously employed only verses of seven, eight, ten, and twelve syllables may be seen to have closural importance: "... meter is a force for closure only when it ceases to function as a pure systematic repetition" (Smith, p. 43). According to the author of *Poetic Closure,*

> ... if the poet wishes to disturb the reader's complacent expectation of continuation (either for closure or for any other reason), one of the most effective devices he could use would be simply a longer or shorter line. (pp. 43–44)

But the *rime en écho* is not inevitably a closural mechanism in the *Fables.* In some cases (see IV, 11; VII, 1; IX, 16) it functions effectively at other spots within poems.

La Fontaine sometimes has recourse to "closural allusions" (for examples, see Smith, pp. 172–82), strongly hinting that the poem is about to end. In "La Cour du lion" (VII, 6), he makes clear that he intends to summarize the import of the anecdote:

> Ceci vous sert d'enseignement:
> Ne soyez à la cour, si vous voulez y plaire,
> Ni fade adulateur, ni parleur trop sincère;
> Et tâchez quelquefois de répondre en Normand.

Although the fabulist appears to be concluding resolutely, the rhyme of *enseignement* with *Normand* (given the context) creates a kind of semantic tension: "On dit qu'un homme répond en Normand lorsqu'il ne dit ni oui ni non, qu'il a crainte d'être surpris, de s'engager" (Furetière, quoted by Couton: *F,* p. 470, n. 9). Perhaps the true lesson is that cheap advice is never worth much and that readers would be well advised not to rely on succinctly expressed poetic formulas. Perhaps, in other words, the narrator himself is replying "en Normand" to those appealing for guidance as to appropriate conduct at court. A similar allusion to the approaching end appears in the final lines of "Le Rat et l'huître" (VIII, 9):

> Cette Fable contient plus d'un enseignement.
>   Nous y voyons premièrement:
> Que ceux qui n'ont du monde aucune expérience
> Sont aux moindres objets frappés d'étonnement:
>   Et puis nous y pouvons apprendre,
>   Que tel est pris qui croyait prendre.

According to Odette de Mourgues, this concluding six-line passage "assure l'équilibre parfait du poème."[7] De Mourgues explains why, in her view, the *morale* here is so effective:

Elle rétablit notre sens des proportions normales du monde: nous quittons un univers dominé par des taupinières, peuplé d'huîtres géantes et nous retrouvons notre taille d'homme. Le ton neutre de cette morale nous rappelle que, si touchante que puisse être la naïveté juvénile, l'étonnement n'est en fait qu'un manque d'expérience, lequel est désastreux. Enfin, pour qu'il n'y ait pas le moindre risque que la mort cruelle du rat provoque en nous un attendrissement ou un moment d'effroi incompatibles avec le comique, le dernier vers de la morale, délibérément sec, réduit le destin tragique de l'animal à une formule abstraite

qui traduit le mouvement antithétique des lois naturelles.
(p. 182)

Such an adroit discussion of these verses helps to justify
their inclusion in the poem and to blunt possible charges
that the fabulist is engaging here in discursive overkill. It
could be reasonably argued that the four preceding lines,
which recount the demise of the outmatched rodent of
the title ("Rat de peu de cervelle"), provide adequate closure:

> Là-dessus maître Rat plein de belle espérance,
> Approche de l'écaille, allonge un peu le cou,
> Se sent pris comme aux lacs; car l'Huître tout d'un coup
> Se referme, et voilà ce que fait l'ignorance.

As de Mourgues indicates, the appended conclusion reas-
sesses the import of the anecdote on the human level,
though this is always the reader's implicit frame of reference in contemplating the action of any fable. The other
elements of the six-line ending are all apparent in the episode itself. Early in the poem, wonder and obvious inex-
perience are nicely fused when the rat involuntarily reveals a deficient sense of geography: "Voilà les Apennins,
et voici le Caucase: / La moindre taupinée était mont à ses
yeux." Similarly, another of the rat's mistaken references
to his wide travels ("Pour moi, j'ai déjà vu le maritime
empire"), considering the reader's knowledge of the
source of the utterance, ". . . sonne creux, souligne l'attitude pompeuse du jeune prétentieux, mais en même
temps exprime aussi admirablement une réaction d'émer-
veillement de la part du rat" (de Mourgues, p. 180). As the
critic maintains, the final line of the fable—"Que tel est pris
qui croyait prendre"—succeeds in removing any possibility that the event will be viewed in a tragic light. But for
that matter the curtly dismissive tag, "et voilà ce que fait

l'ignorance," has already performed the same service. Furthermore, the tone of the entire poem has worked to ensure that the reader will not fall prey to any emotions "incompatibles avec le comique." Whether or not one approves the overtness of the concluding lines, they do provide memorable phrases describing the fable's underlying ironic structure: the rat's confident unawareness of danger caused him to become the oyster's quick meal, the fitness of his fate being enhanced by a wry reversal of subject and object ("C'est quelque victuaille," the rat had exclaimed upon spying the oyster, but the intended food would soon consume the would-be consumer).

Twentieth-century readers, accustomed to poetry featuring subtlety, ambiguity, open-ended finales and various kinds of misdirection, are likely to find somewhat ponderous or inartistic all endings that overtly signal their closural intent. In the *Fables,* the aphoristic résumé, whatever its form, is seldom if ever as esthetically satisfying a means of securing closure as more oblique strategies. Rarely, however, is formal cessation unaccompanied by a sense of completeness. The definition of "hidden closure" proposed by Barbara Herrnstein Smith is helpful:

> . . . while anti-closure in modern poetry is a recognizable tendency with interesting consequences, it is rarely realized as the total absence of closural effects. The tendency reveals itself primarily in what might be called "hidden closure," where the poet will avoid the expressive qualities of strong closure while securing, in various ways, the reader's sense of the poem's integrity. (p. 244)

Although the closure in many of the fables is hidden, it is not irretrievably buried. The more indirect its thrust, however, the greater the challenge to the explicator seeking clues to a poem's global meaning. The presence of a maxim never dictates that the reader's quest for poetic meaning must begin and end there, but the absence of a

nugget of proverbial wisdom removes a convenient interpretive starting point while inviting the reader to comb
the entire text assiduously in a search for signs of coherence permitting a retrospective justification of the ending.
The principle can best be understood by a close consideration of interesting examples.

Let us begin by examining "Le Loup et le chien" (I, 5),
a poem that traditionally has been read as a statement in
praise of liberty. It is not at all difficult, of course, to
marshal arguments in support of this view. The idea that
freedom is precious had been explicitly conveyed in earlier fables about the wolf and the dog. The moral is omit-
ted from La Fontaine's version, but one might argue that
the lesson was so obvious to him that to express it would
have been superfluous. In his preface to the *Fables* of
1668, La Fontaine states that he had left the moral out of
poems only "dans les endroits où elle n'a pu entrer avec
grâce, et où il est aisé au lecteur de la suppléer" (*F*, p. 10).
In reading "Le Loup et le chien" one is indeed tempted to
supply the moral given by the French fabulist's predecessors.

The import of this fable about the wolf who decides
that he would rather be free and hungry than forced to
wear a collar and work for an owner has certainly seemed
clear to critics. The editors of the Bordas edition of the
Fables beg the question of the poem's theme by asking,
"Cette fable est-elle la seule où La Fontaine ait exprimé
son goût pour la liberté?"[8] Authors of literary manuals cite
"Le Loup et le chien" as an illustration of La Fontaine's
preoccupation with the theme of liberty.[9] One frequently
encounters fuller studies of La Fontaine that make essentially the same point. Pierre Bornecque believes this fable
to be one of four in Book I that develop "le thème de la
liberté"; in this instance the fabulist is said to illustrate the
notion that "dans la pauvreté elle [liberty] est préférable à
l'esclavage dans la richesse."[10] Renée Kohn claims that in
"Le Loup et le chien" the poet's sympathy is directed to the

heroism of the wolf and that, at the end of the fable, one has the impression that liberty has triumphed forever.[11] Similarly, René Jasinski maintains that in this fable the poet sides with the wolf against the dog.[12] Jean-Pierre Collinet finds in this poem "un dilemme entre l'indépendance farouche et la dégradante acceptation de la servitude. . . ."[13] In an entertaining article on "Le Loup et le chien," Stirling Haig considers the interplay of alexandrines and octosyllables in this poem to be significant. At the outset the fabulist introduces what Haig calls a "hunger-weakened, octosyllabic wolf" and "a splendidly sleek alexandrine dog." But he claims that a shift occurs in the last four lines of the poem, a reversal that pictures the wolf "in his new alexandrine independence."[14] For Stirling Haig, even the poem's metric pattern underscores the implied moral. Susan Tiefenbrun also stresses the wolf's liberty, though with comparative restraint, when she focuses on a "point of ironic reversal" at which the poem "pivots . . . away from the enslavement of court security toward the qualified merits of political and social freedom."[15] Jules Brody's brilliant reading of the poem generally moves in the same direction, I think, but his exploration of the fable's linguistic texture goes well beyond such discursive, paraphrasable elements as "Liberty is precious" or "Servitude is never sweet."[16]

Without question these critics have emphasized an important aspect of the fable. But, as I tried to establish in an article published several years ago, such interpretations have not uncovered the poem's full meaning.[17] This viewpoint is to an extent corroborated by David Lee Rubin's analysis of "Le Loup et le chien" in his essay on "double irony" in the *Fables;* having discovered greater complexity in the language of the poem than has traditionally been acknowledged, Rubin states: "This undercutting of the ostensibly correct interpretation suggests that there may even be grounds for a paradoxical case— *against* the wolf and *for* the dog."[18] Despite appearances, the poetic truth of this fable is not one-sided. Those who consider only the wolf's viewpoint may be missing a very basic principle: that what is a perfectly natural course of action for the wolf might be disastrous for the dog. In other words, life in the wilderness may be fine for those who are accustomed to such a rude existence, but calamitous for those who are domesticated. In attempting to make a case for the dog's possible perspective, I will first provide a thematic framework for his position by referring to other poems in the first six books of the *Fables* (published in 1668) that appear to be in some ways analogous. Then I will examine more closely the text of "Le Loup et le chien" itself, before finally showing what might be viewed as ironic implications of the poem's closure.

In interpreting the *Fables* one would be unwise to stop at the level of simple statement. Nonetheless, a cautious reading of thematic elements from poem to poem often can prove instructive, enabling the critic to perceive patterns that acquire added prominence through repetition or transmutation. One of the most frequently repeated themes of the 1668 collection is that we should be satisfied with what we have. It is the overt lesson of "La Grenouille qui se veut faire aussi grosse que le boeuf" (I, 3), in which a frog explodes while trying to emulate an ox. In "Le Corbeau voulant imiter l'aigle" (II, 16), a crow is captured after trying to carry off a sheep as an eagle had done. The fabulist explains the poem's ostensible import in this manner: "Il faut se mesurer, la conséquence est nette: / Mal prend aux Volereaux de faire les Voleurs." As if the sense were not already clear, he adds:

> L'exemple est un dangereux leurre:
> Tous les mangeurs de gens ne sont pas grands Seigneurs;
> Où la Guêpe a passé, le Moucheron demeure.

The peacock in "Le Paon se plaignant à Junon" (II, 17) is

envious of the nightingale's lovely song. He learns from Junon, however, that he should be grateful for his plumage, because "Tout animal n'a pas toutes propriétés. / Nous vous avons donné diverses qualités." Unlike the inflated frog, the ambitious crow or the envious peacock, the dog in "Le Loup et le chien" appears to be perfectly contented with his situation, even though a collar has chafed his neck bare.

The lesson that one ought to be happy with what one possesses emerges in many other forms in the fables of 1668. The frogs in "Les Grenouilles qui demandent un roi" (III, 4), having grown tired of democracy, ask Jupin (a burlesque rendition of Jupiter) to give them a king. Having received a wooden beam as monarch, they complain again, asking Jupin to send them "un roi qui se remue." This time they are given a crane, "Qui les croque, qui les tue, / Qui les gobe à son plaisir." What is the declared moral? That the frogs should have accepted their original government. Since they rejected democracy, says Jupin, "il vous devait suffire / Que votre premier roi fût débonnaire et doux." Now they are stuck with a frog-eating bird-king, but Jupin tells them they should not ask to change monarchs again, "De peur d'en rencontrer un pire." In a similar manner, the ass in "L'Ane et ses maîtres" (VI, 11) regrets having asked fate to give him a new master. The fabulist's observation—"Notre condition jamais ne nous contente: / La pire est toujours la présente" —implies again that one should accept whatever one has. In "Le Bûcheron et Mercure" (V, 1), the woodcutter is rewarded by Mercury precisely because he is satisfied with what he possesses. After having lost his hatchet, he turns down a gold one and then a silver one before identifying as his own a hatchet made of wood. What lesson does the narrator offer? "Ne point mentir, être content du sien, / C'est le plus sûr. . . ." "Le Berger et la mer" (IV, 2) is a fable that illustrates the danger of speculation. The author shows "Qu'un sou, quand il est assuré, / Vaut mieux que

cinq en espérance; / Qu'il se faut contenter de sa condition." The dog in "Le Loup et le chien," opting as he does
for security (albeit not devoid of drawbacks), is one creature in La Fontaine's poetic universe who appears to have
taken such advice to heart.

Again and again the fabulist in his narrative voice emphasizes the importance of living in conformity with
one's nature. "L'Ane et le petit chien" (IV, 5) opens with
these lines:

> Ne forçons point notre talent,
> Nous ne ferions rien avec grâce:
> Jamais un lourdaud, quoi qu'il fasse,
> Ne saurait passer pour galant.

A bumpkin is never a fashionable gentleman, a frog is not
an ox, nor is a domesticated dog a wild wolf. And an
earthen pot is quite different from an iron pot. Everyone
familiar with the *Fables* will no doubt recall the moral of
"Le Pot de terre et le pot de fer" (V, 2), announced after
the earthen pot has been literally shattered by his companion:

> Ne nous associons qu'avecque nos égaux.
> Ou bien il nous faudra craindre
> Le destin d'un de ces Pots.

The poet likewise calls attention to individual differences
in "L'Ane chargé d'éponges, et l'âne chargé de sel" (II,
10). The salt-donkey's load lightens as the salt melts in a
river he is crossing. The sponge-donkey, on the other
hand, nearly drowns when, imitating his companion, he
plunges into the water. The lesson proposed here is that
". . . il ne faut point / Agir chacun de même sorte." Could
the plump household dog in "Le Loup et le chien" survive
among wolves in the forest? It is more likely, I believe, that
he would be as helpless as the earthen pot or the sponge-

donkey if left to his own devices in the wilderness. Admittedly, the hypothesis is unprovable, just as it cannot be ascertained whether Chimène will ever marry Rodrigue. The text is always a solid boundary dividing interpretation from pure speculation. My point is only that the text of "Le Loup et le chien" appears to invite a critical reading that takes into account the importance of individualism from the perspective of each character.

The theme of liberty in La Fontaine is by no means a static, univalent concept, constant in its applicability to people and animals in all times, places, and situations. Yet Pierre Clarac, in his *Connaissance des Lettres* study of La Fontaine, cites this frequently quoted passage from "Le Cheval s'étant voulu venger du cerf" (IV, 13)—that liberty is ". . . un bien / Sans qui les autres ne sont rien"—as evidence of the poet's "passion de la liberté." Clarac also suggests that there is a thematic relationship between this fable and "Le Loup et le chien."[19] From the wolf's point of view there is clearly a parallel, but the dog in "Le Loup et le chien" is not really similar to the horse in "Le Cheval s'étant voulu venger du cerf." We are told early in the latter fable that horses used to roam free in forests. But once a horse went to a man for assistance after attempting without success to catch a stag on which he wanted to gain vengeance. The man bridled the horse, jumped on his back and would not let him rest until the stag was captured. Then the man decided to keep the horse as a domestic animal. The narrator exclaims: "Hélas! que sert la bonne chère / Quand on n'a pas la liberté?"—a lament that echoes our wolf's final tirade. The horse "s'aperçut qu'il avait fait folie," but his freedom was gone forever. He died in his stable "en traînant son lien." This is the somber context in which liberty is praised as ". . . un bien / Sans qui les autres ne sont rien." At first glance, this fable may appear to be analogous to "Le Loup et le chien." In both cases, freedom for animals seems to be preferred to domestication. But the dog never claims to desire freedom. On the other hand, the horse says to the man after catching the stag, "Je m'en retourne en mon séjour sauvage." This is in the order of things for animals like the horse and the wolf, who are depicted as being accustomed to living in the woods. Animals (or people, or pots) should follow their nature; they should be satisfied with their personal status quo. This point, emphasized (as we have seen) in numerous fables, is restated in different terms in "Le Cheval s'étant voulu venger du cerf." For the horse, "se contenter de sa condition" would have meant to forgo revenge and to stay in the forest. But the dog in "Le Loup et le chien" has no desire to be rid of his confinement. He has probably never known the liberty that the horse once enjoyed, and he would in all likelihood be incapable of coping with freedom in the wilderness even if he had the opportunity to romp away with the wolf. (In fact, the option to flee does exist because he is collarless at the time of the conversation.) As I will now attempt to demonstrate, nothing in the text of "Le Loup et le chien" contradicts the line of reasoning in which the dog's existential position is judged to be as valid on its own terms as that of the wolf.

Early in the fable, the dog is described as "puissant," "beau," "gras," and "poli." He is apparently thriving in captivity. When complimented on his "embonpoint," he says that by abandoning the woods the wolf will be able to become as stout as he is. The dog paints a bleak picture of what he imagines to be the life-style of wolves in the forest:

> Vos pareils y sont misérables,
> Cancres, haires, et pauvres diables,
> Dont la condition est de mourir de faim.

Out there in the woods, claims the dog, there are no free meals ("point de franche lippée"); you have to fight for everything you get ("Tout à la pointe de l'épée"). One would surely have to read between the lines to agree with

Renée Kohn that "L'opposition de ces deux mots rabelaisi-
ens, épais et matériels 'franche lippée,' et du vers vibrant et net, chevaleresque et hardi: 'Tout à la pointe de
l'épée,' "[20] somehow reveals the poet's sympathy for the
heroism of wolves. It is interesting that the wolf neither
alters this description of life in the wilderness nor praises
his fellow wolves for their courage. When told that by
imitating the dog he can have a better fate, the wolf, evidently finding the prospect appealing, asks straightfor-
wardly, "Que me faudra-t-il faire?" "Presque rien," answers the dog. He does not suggest in any way that his
duties are arduous or that he would prefer to earn his living
in another way. He merely lists his responsibilities without
commenting on them: ". . . donner la chasse aux gens /
Portants bâtons, et mendiants; / Flatter ceux du logis, à son
maître complaire." Privately, the reader may have a very
low opinion of individuals who spend their time in such
activities, but one's general attitude toward beggar-chasing
sycophants is beside the point. What does this wolf seem
to think about such a life? He starts to weep and "se forge
une félicité" upon learning that he will be rewarded for
performing these tasks. It is only when he notices the dog's
chafed neck that the wolf changes his mind about the
benefits of civilization. There is nothing in the dog's answers to the wolf's rapid-fire questions that would seem to
reveal any sadness or any longing for the open spaces. The
wolf wonders at first what he has accidentally discovered:
"Chemin faisant, il vit le col du Chien pelé. / Qu'est-ce là?
lui dit-il." When asked what he has on his neck, the dog
replies simply, "Rien." The wolf persists: "Quoi? rien?"
"Peu de chose," the dog answers. But the wolf refuses to
drop the subject: "Mais encor?" At this point the dog reveals the whole truth about his neck: "Le collier dont je suis
attaché / De ce que vous voyez est peut-être la cause."
(Though he habitually wears a collar he is not confined at
present; "Chemin faisant" with the wolf, he is on furlough
from his duties.) If the dog's hesitation prior to his full

revelation implies embarrassment, such an emotion is not reflected by the words he uses in telling of the collar; the language is direct and dispassionate. As might be expected, the wolf finds this disclosure terribly shocking. "Attaché?" he cries; "vous ne courez donc pas / Où vous voulez?" The dog responds simply, "Pas toujours, mais qu'importe?" It is difficult to understand how Renée Kohn was able to determine that this reply is delivered "avec un ton inimitable de lassitude et de tristesse," or how Pierre Moreau was able to discern the "voix embarrassée" of the dog.[21] The poem is of course potentially dramatic in that it is composed in large measure of a dialogue. But if the fable were to become a mini-drama, with actors playing the parts of wolf and dog, the lines could be delivered in various ways. In the absence of further evidence, the dog does not appear to be necessarily either tired or sad. He has a good thing going, despite the possible inconvenience of being frequently collared. Confinement is the only life he knows, and he accepts it without regret. Quite understandably, this kind of existence fails to appeal to the wolf. At the end of the fable he naturally chooses to keep his freedom, even though he has not solved the problem of getting enough to eat. But he does not ask the dog to join him. The stated moral of "Le Cheval et le loup" (V, 8)—"Chacun à son métier doit toujours s'attacher"—seems applicable to "Le Loup et le chien" as well. The dog wisely accepts his condition, just as the wolf opts for his natural state.

As indicated earlier, La Fontaine's predecessors clearly stated what they considered to be the theme of the fable of the wolf and the dog. For instance, the first words of the "Lupus ad Canem" of Phaedrus are these: "How sweet liberty is I will briefly declare."[22] And in Millot's French translation of Aesop's fables, the following moral appears at the end of the fable that, according to René Jasinski, is the most direct source of "Le Loup et le chien": "La fable enseigne combien la liberté est douce, et que tous les biens du monde ne lui sont pas comparables."[23] On the other hand, no moral is expressed in La Fontaine's version of the fable. Did the writer wish to build ambiguity into the poem? Did he think the lesson was so clear that stating it would be pointless? Any effort to reconstruct the poet's possible reasons for omitting the moral would be futile. Like any literary work, "Le Loup et le chien" has an existence independent of earlier renditions of the anecdote on which it is based and independent as well of the author's private interpretation of the poem—a matter that relates to significance rather than to meaning. Even if La Fontaine had adorned the poem with a moral, it might not have been the best one possible. Even if appropriate, it could not have expressed fully the meaning of the fable. But solving problems of closure never involves examining ways in which a work does not end. How does "Le Loup et le chien" actually conclude?

After hearing the dog admit that he cannot always wander where he pleases ("Pas toujours, mais qu'importe?"), the wolf exclaims:

> —Il importe si bien, que de tous vos repas
> Je ne veux en aucune sorte,
> Et ne voudrais pas même à ce prix un trésor.

Thereupon the narrator adds a final alexandrine: "Cela dit, maître Loup s'enfuit, et court encor." For Jules Brody, the appellation *maître,* which replaces earlier references to the wolf as "Sire Loup" and "beau Sire," is noteworthy:

> Thanks to the strand that surfaces with *à son maître com-plaire,* the ensuing *Maître Loup s'enfuit* is able to mark the terminus of a linguistic continuum, taking on a semantic surplus large enough to transform the perfunctory rhetorical epithet into a functioning ironic sign. In this last line, the native, latent content of the word *maître* is activated and as this happens it becomes ironically and poetically efficient, in that it now *does* more than it *says.*[24]

This interpretation reinforces Brody's fascinating argument that the poem's initial line, "Un Loup n'avait que les os et la peau," is transformed by subsequent images of skin and bones concerning the two title characters: "As a function of skin-and-bones and nothingness, one has become the other" (p. 85). Though the wolf's exit fittingly terminates the fable (the opposed viewpoints having been adequately developed , and their irreconcilability confirmed), it is uncertain that his perpetual running denotes mastership. Will his endless lope lead him to a little hard-earned nourishment, or will he turn out to be just another of those unfortunate creatures out in the wilds "Dont la condition est de mourir de faim"? No one can say. Losses and gains in this poem are not easily tallied. David Lee Rubin may well be correct when he asserts that ". . . the only closure or sense of finality that the fable possesses is formal" rather than ideological.[25] Formally, a sense of at least tentative conclusiveness is perceptible: the final rhymed alexandrine couplet contrasts with the prosodic arrangement of the preceding four lines (verses of three lengths connected in *rime croisée*); a fairly long spoken passage is succeeded by a brief narrative report; the statement that the wolf "court encor" virtually precludes additional revelations about his destiny. In dialectic terms, however, the entire poem "court encor" as resolutely as the wolf. As Rubin maintains,

> . . . the conflict between viewpoints [is] never satisfactorily resolved. Interpretation after undercutting interpretation can and surely will be made without end. However unstable the irony of the fable is, there is no wandering away from the ostensible subject matter, the problematic of freedom and constraint. In the end, it may well be this problematic, nothing more nor less, that La Fontaine seeks to disclose to the reader in a text which makes a major deviation from "classic" irony. (p. 206)

The lack of tendentiousness in Rubin's commentary, capturing the openness of the fable with cogent clarity, is a most refreshing departure from typical readings that insist on wedging La Fontaine's poetry into deceptively well-illuminated compartments of paraphrase. The irony in "Le Loup et le chien" may be local rather than infinite, but there is no justification for denying its instability.

If one approaches La Fontaine's fables, even those that appear at first to be self-explanatory, without any preconceived notions of their meaning, the net result will include a better understanding of their dense ironic texture. It would be foolish to advocate the mad pursuit of phantom themes and arcane symbols, but when there is textual support for multi-dimensional interpretations, our appreciation of the fables can be greatly enhanced by recognition of their complexity. Another poem that raises pertinent issues of irony and closure while rewarding an impartial approach to possible meanings is "Le Satyre et le passant" (V, 7). Here, as elsewhere, a basic aspect of the explicator's assignment will be to examine what Odette de Mourgues has called the fabulist's "art of leaving something unsaid, the art of selection and sacrifice."[26]

On a narrative level, this twenty-eight-line poem, presented in heptasyllabic quatrains, is quite straightforward. A satyr and his family are about to have some soup when a passerby, chilled and eager to escape the rain, enters their den. Having accepted an invitation to share their meal, he blows first on his fingers to warm them and then on his soup to make it cool. When the passerby explains how his breath is doubly useful, the satyr, astonished and troubled by this behavior, promptly asks the visitor to leave.

In the first line of the poem the satyr and his family are placed "au fond d'un antre sauvage." As the episode unfolds it will become evident that psychologically as well as physically the satyr dwells in the dark. We soon learn that his manners are as primitive as his den: he and his children "allaient manger leur potage / Et prendre l'écuelle aux dents"; he, his wife and their large brood ("maint petit") dine "sur la mousse," having no cover on which to put their food, "mais tous fort bon appétit." The narrator reveals very little to us about these creatures, emphasizing in this brief introduction (lines 1–8) scarcely more than their survival instinct. Nothing mentioned here would prompt us to believe that they are lucid thinkers prone to inferring symbolic significance from events.

In the following stanza the passerby arrives. The poet provides only information required to advance the story: the visitor is "morfondu," enters the cave because it is raining outside, quickly accepts an invitation to have soup with the family. At this point the visitor inadvertently prepares his abrupt departure. His battle with the weather has left him chilled to the bone, so at the outset "avec son haleine / Il se réchauffe les doigts." Without commenting on this action the narrator adds, "Puis sur le mets qu'on lui donne / Délicat il souffle aussi." These actions are described almost without evaluative language. The only term possibly conveying the narrator's attitude toward the scene is *délicat*, which in the seventeenth century could carry this pejorative sense: "D'une sensibilité excessive en matière de goût, de plaisir."[27] Even if the passerby is being criticized for his fastidiousness, however, these lines do not extend an invitation to treat the incident as allegory.

The satyr is nonetheless puzzled by this unassuming display of versatility. He "s'en étonne" and asks the visitor, "à quoi bon ceci?" Without hesitation the latter answers: "L'un refroidit mon potage, / L'autre réchauffe ma main." That is all. There is no reference to any hidden thoughts he may be harboring, no indication that the narrator is aware of a fuller, symbolic sense. In other words, in the absence of an explicit or implicit context it is difficult to find grounds for considering the passerby's response ironic. Yet the satyr refuses to accept this literal explanation of the cooling and warming capabilities of breath: "Vous pouvez, dit le Sauvage, / Reprendre votre chemin." Primitive he is indeed, a suitable occupant of the "antre sauvage" of line one, his mind's "objective correlative." Possessing not even the most rudimentary notions of jurisprudence or fair play, he dismisses the passerby without giving him an opportunity to elaborate. Judge and jury, the satyr rounds out the fable by way of a brief monologue introduced by the request that the visitor leave the cave and concluded by this quatrain:

> Ne plaise aux Dieux que je couche
> Avec vous sous même toit.
> Arrière ceux dont la bouche
> Souffle le chaud et le froid!

His assessment of the situation is perfectly in character. All that we know about him (taking "l'écuelle aux dents," having "fort bon appétit") confirms that his life is body-oriented; he is initially hospitable to the passerby, but not (quite understandably) to the extent of going hungry himself. Given the portrait of the satyr created in the poem, it would be hard to argue persuasively that he has a keen intellect. And the lack of such clues is in itself an aid to explication. To paraphrase Samuel Beckett's reaction to the perennial theory that Godot is God, if La Fontaine had intended that the satyr be judged perceptive, he would somehow have said so—in the poem. Since he has not conveyed this idea, even by implication, it is necessary to base any judgment on what the text of "Le Satyre et le passant" does tell us, the poet's private intentions (whatever they may have been) and the direct moral pronouncements of the fable's literary models being irrelevant.

In a characteristically succinct formula, Pierre Bornecque states what he believes to be the poem's theme: "honneur à la loyauté et honte à l'hypocrisie!"[28] One is reminded of René Jasinski's interpretation of the fable, for he, too, sides unequivocally with the satyr:

> Comment ne pas prendre parti pour le héros, simple et bon, patriarcalement entouré de sa famille dans sa caverne, prêt à partager son repas avec l'étranger de passage, et pris d'une répulsion presque physique devant la seule idée de l'hypocrisie?[29]

The viewpoint of these critics is finally not convincing because their account of the poem's meaning is inadequately substantiated by textual evidence. The fable's import, however interpreted, seems to have almost nothing to do with loyalty (except insofar as the satyr's retraction of hospitality may disqualify him from being called loyal), nor does the satyr merit our viewing him as heroic by any conventional standards of heroism. Furthermore, the very mention of hypocrisy is an intrusion of the reader's conceptual system into the world of the satyr. To suggest, as Jasinski does, that the satyr finds hypocrisy repugnant is to imply that the character is capable of abstract thinking—an assumption the text does not permit us to make. A more plausible explanation of the satyr's reaction to his guest's two-way talent is, in my opinion, that the basis of the response must be largely sensory. The satyr is probably incapable of intellectualizing experience. His view of life is shaped by the messages of the physical senses. Never before, one supposes, has he encountered someone whose breath served both to warm and to cool. Although he may not have the mental capacity to regard the dual effect of the passerby's blowing as a sign of duplicity, he certainly possesses the brute instinct to survive and to avoid misfortune (he lives sheltered from the elements; when hungry he eats). Central to this instinct is a fear of the unknown or at least a vague uneasiness about anything that seems mysterious. The stranger's behavior denotes the unknown and the satyr feels the instinctive need to send the visitor away, even if he cannot verbalize a rationale for this desire. Since life has not taught him that breath can fill a double function, he imagines that what he has just witnessed somehow involves trickery. It does not occur to him to pursue the matter further. What this non-Cartesian mistakenly assumes to be common sense will suffice, together with a dash of superstition ("Ne plaise aux Dieux que je couche / Avec vous sous même toit").[30]

Whereas the satyr's error lies in his failure to comprehend observable acts, literary critics are more likely to fall prey to overexplication—a tendency to invent and probe the unobserved. As the poem stands, there is no justification for saying, with Jasinski, that it illustrates that "il faut déjouer les pièges de ceux-là mêmes à qui nous faisons du bien" (II, 204). What *pièges?* There is no indication in the poem that the passerby is pernicious or deceptive. We do not know where he was going, or why, when he took refuge in the satyr's den. We have no idea what he might have done had he been permitted to stay there. We do not know these things because his life begins and ends with the poem. The fate of the characters in "Le Satyre et le passant" is as fixed—in the perpetual present tense of art—as the destiny of the figures on Keats's Grecian urn. Horace kills Camille again and again; she dies yet never dies. Freed of the real-world exigencies of space and time and biology, the satyr and his guest are forever caught in the Sisyphean situation of performing the same tasks anew for each reader. No other tasks will they ever perform. René Jasinski charges that the passerby "joue un double jeu" (II, 206), but the satyr discloses no information that would make an accusation of hypocrisy stick.

As it happens, the satyr is related, by behavior if not by blood, to many characters in the *Fables*, those victims of irony who are incapable of distinguishing appearance from reality. Such a victim indeed appears in the first fable of Book I: the singing cicada who does not comprehend the harsh reality of seasonal changes.[31] Similarly, the animals in society with the lion (I, 6) fail to understand the reality of authoritarian leonine conduct; the horse, encountered some pages ago, in "Le Cheval s'étant voulu venger du cerf" (IV, 13) is unaware of the dangers of asking man for assistance; the briefly triumphant rooster in "Les Deux Coqs" (VII, 12) learns, as he pridefully heralds his victory, that it has been but a Pyrrhic success ("Tout cet orgueil périt sous l'ongle du Vautour"); in "Le Loup et le chien maigre" (IX, 10), the wolf comprehends only too late that there is no profit in waiting. The world of the *Fables* is filled with such characters. The satyr offers an interesting variation of the cases just cited. Whereas the cicada, the lion's associates, the horse, the rooster, and the wolf all consider illusion to be truth, the satyr's problem is the reverse: in his visceral response to an uncomplicated occurrence he mistakes reality for appearance. We probe the poem in vain for hints, however subtle, that the visitor's blowing means more than he claims. He puffs on his fingers merely to relieve his discomfort; he blows on his soup solely to avoid burning his tongue. It is his misfortune to have encountered a host who, like today's legions of professional scandalmongers, cannot—or will not—accept these normal, unmysterious actions for what they are. Just as the satyr draws his bowl to his mouth without bothering to use a spoon, so he reacts hastily and instinctively to the gestures of his guest without raising arguments that would favor, or at least admit, a literal interpretation of them. He is as single-minded as the vengeful wolf in "Le Loup et l'agneau" (I, 10) who, having ignored the lamb's reasonable protestations of innocence, carries his victim deep into the forest "et puis le mange, / Sans autre forme de procès." To be sure, the passerby is not martyred but only inconvenienced. He is not the focal point of the reader's emotions. We sympathize with him only to the extent that he is the unwitting object of the satyr's misapprehension of circumstances. Our ultimate reaction in reading the poem centers upon the ridiculousness of the satyr, whom La Fontaine allows to be muddle-headed with impunity. "Arrière ceux dont la bouche / Souffle le chaud et le froid!": these lines provide successful closure without calling excessive attention to their terminal qualities. This is one of the rare fables in which La Fontaine does not allow himself the option of securing closure partly through prosodic modification: lines of seven syllables and the *abab* rhyming pattern are preserved throughout. Here the closural elements are semantic and thematic. According to Smith, "A high incidence of formal parallelism and antithesis obviously tends to produce what we call 'epigrammatic' effects; and when such devices occur at the conclusion of a poem they also have striking closural force" (p. 171). The antithetical terms *chaud* and *froid* summarize an opposition woven into the poem's linguistic fabric and still unresolved: *(se) réchauffe* on one side, *morfondu* and *refroidit* on the other, *haleine* and *souffle* bridging the gap. Though he seems blissfully unaware of the parallel, in his final words the satyr describes the warmth and coldness of his own verbal conduct while totally misjudging the other man's actions: the satyr's initial cordiality has become frigid as he is now on the verge of expelling the traveler. Finally, the noun *bouche* recalls the principal activities of all the characters (the satyr and his children are first identified by the verb *manger* and by the noun *dents;* the visitor is memorable for his *haleine)* while perhaps evoking the *antre sauvage* of line one—metaphorically not the misunderstood passerby's mouth, but the satyr's.

Some will possibly think they detect in my analysis a certain new-critical stubbornness, troubling symptoms of exegetical tunnel-vision. What this little anecdote was traditionally supposed to mean is indisputable. In his rendition of the fable, Millot (thought by Jasinski to be La Fontaine's closest model) concludes with this unequivocal tag-line: "La fable signifie qu'il faut fuir l'amitié de ceux qui sont doubles et variables" (quoted in Jasinski, II, 205). But the study of sources has limited usefulness for the explicator. It can show us the degree to which La Fontaine is imitative or original and it can illustrate his talent for bringing to life the often flat, overexplicit materials of his predecessors. But we cannot explicate La Fontaine's fables by dealing with his models any more fruitfully than we can discover the import of *Le Cid* by consulting Guilhem de Castro or that of *La Machine infernale* by studying Sophocles. "Le Satyre et le passant" cannot be forced to carry meanings that are without internal basis, direct or inferential. Jasinski disagrees with judgments made by Voltaire ("le satyre était un sot") and by Chamfort ("la duplicité d'un homme qui dit tantôt une chose et tantôt une autre n'a rien de commun avec cette conduite" of the passerby in the fable) (II, 204). But it seems to me that the interpretations adumbrated by these eighteenth-century writers indicate that both of them evaluated the poem's internal evidence more assiduously than the modern critics Jasinski and Bornecque.

"Le Satyre et le passant" effectively illustrates the principle of "selection and sacrifice," to borrow again Odette de Mourgues's felicitous phrase. In this fable, La Fontaine has selected details that characterize the satyr as a primitive governed not by intellect but by appetite while sacrificing details (found in earlier fables on the same theme) that would invite us to view the visitor as a hypocrite. Needless to say, La Fontaine is a skillful writer fully capable of supplying clues to the interpretation of his poetry. By sacrificing certain clues in "Le Satyre et le passant" and by selecting others, he demonstrates that his "imitation n'est point un esclavage" (*OD*, p. 648), and he enhances the esthetic value of an old aphoristic story by encouraging—and amply rewarding—a slow, attentive reading of his poem.

The concept of esthetic sacrifice activated in the *Fables* helps to liberate these poems from the overdiscursiveness

of their millennial heritage. David H. Richter's differenti-
ation between two kinds of apologues appears to shed
some light on the typical functioning of the moral dimension in the *Fables*. Richter establishes his distinction of
apologue types with reference to two biblical stories:

> The parable of the tares is in the allegorical mode; that is,
> there is set up a one-to-one correspondence between ob-
> jects and characters in the fiction and beings, persons, and
> ideas in the real world external to the fiction.

No fable of La Fontaine exhibits a meaning so tightly cir-
cumscribed. On the other hand, many (perhaps all) of his
fables are truly "fables" in the sense proposed by Richter:

> . . . the parable of the good Samaritan is a fable, a rhetori-
> cal fiction in which each detail of plot, characterization,
> and language is chosen in order to make us understand
> something in the external world . . . but in which the indi-
> vidual details generally do not have symbolic significance
> that can be detached from the fiction and equated on a
> one-for-one basis with ideas in the external world.[32]

Although Richter is dealing in his book with "rhetorical
fiction" (ranging from *Rasselas* and *Candide* to *Lord of the
Flies* and *Catch-22*), his basic definitions are clearly applicable to lyric apologues as well. What Richter terms "fable" seems to be the kind of apologue that Philip A.
Wadsworth has called "allegory." For instance, Wadsworth's discussion of "Le Loup et l'agneau" (I, 10) concludes: "The moral is not a simple statement either in the
first line or the last, but a cluster of ideas which are
presented poetically throughout the fable as a whole."[33]
As Wadsworth indicates, "The allegorical design of fables, once rather rigid and clear, has become extremely
supple and suggestive in the hands of La Fontaine" (p.
1132)—though, strictly speaking, *aphoristic* might be a
more appropriate adjective here than *allegorical*. Similarly,

I would prefer to substitute *moralist* for *allegorist* in Wadsworth's final statement in the article: that "La Fontaine's originality as an allegorist was to create many . . . fables which are rich and provocative and pleasing as expressions of thought" (p. 1135), but his emphasis on the thematic expansiveness of numerous fables of La Fontaine is well placed. Their open qualities often challenge the explicator looking for signs of closural coherence, but the refusal of many of these poems to furnish easily extractable hunks of pith and marrow is an element contributing to their modernity, for in the literature of our own age it would appear that prefabricated answers yield the right of way, more commonly than not, to persistent questions, doubts, and suspension points.

I hope the brief discussion of irony and closure in this chapter has illustrated the importance of examining each fable on its own terms and of considering its full poetic environment. As a few of my comments have suggested, in La Fontaine's poetry, "Beneath the structure, in the texture, is where the *action* is," to cite again Jules Brody's nice phrase. My aim in the next chapter will be to study more closely some ironic implications of texture in the *Fables*.

NOTES

1. *La Philosophie morale des "Fables" de La Fontaine* (Neuchâtel: Editions de la Baconnière, 1951).
2. *La Fontaine: Vues sur l'art du moraliste dans les "Fables" de 1668* (Paris: Société d'Edition "Les Belles Lettres," 1961), pp. 42, 43.
3. *Le Goût de La Fontaine* (Paris: Presses Universitaires de France, 1962), p. 144.
4. Noël Richard, *La Fontaine et les "Fables" du deuxième recueil* (Paris: Nizet, 1972), p. 56.

5. *Qu'est-ce que le classicisme?*, rev. ed. (Paris: Nizet, 1971), p. 129.

6. *Poetic Closure: A Study of How Poems End* (Chicago: Univ. of Chicago Press, 1968), p. 36.

7. *O Muse fuyante proie,* p. 182; see her perceptive analysis of "Le Rat et l'huître," pp. 177–82.

8. Pierre Michel and Maurice Martin, eds., *Fables* (Paris: Bordas, 1964), I, 54.

9. Pierre-Georges Castex and Paul Surer, *Manuel des études littéraires françaises* (Paris: Hachette, 1954), I, 321; André Lagarde and Laurent Michard, *Les Grands Auteurs français du programme: XVIIe siècle* (Paris: Bordas, 1964), p. 238.

10. *La Fontaine fabuliste* (Paris: Société d'Edition d'Enseignement Supérieur, 1973), p. 93.

11. *Le Goût de La Fontaine,* p. 154.

12. *La Fontaine et le premier recueil des "Fables,"* I, 222.

13. *Le Monde littéraire de La Fontaine* (Paris: Presses Universitaires de France, 1970), p. 217.

14. "La Fontaine's 'Le Loup et le chien' as a Pedagogical Instrument," *French Review,'* 42 (1969), 702, 704.

15. "Signs of Irony in La Fontaine's *Fables,*" p. 149.

16. See "Irony in La Fontaine: From Message to Massage," pp. 82–86.

17. Much of the material in these pages first appeared in my essay, "Individualism in La Fontaine's 'Le Loup et le chien,'" *Kentucky Romance Quarterly,* 24 (1977), 185–90.

18. "Four Modes of Double Irony in La Fontaine's *Fables,*" p. 206.

19. *La Fontaine,* new ed. (Paris: Hatier, 1959), p. 78.

20. *Le Goût de La Fontaine,* p. 154.

21. Kohn, p. 154; Moreau, *Thèmes et variations dans le premier recueil des "Fables" de La Fontaine (1668)* (Paris: Centre de Documentation Universitaire, 1960), p. 49.

22. Ben Edwin Perry, trans., *Babrius and Phaedrus* . . . (Cambridge, MA: Harvard Univ. Press, 1965), p. 267.

23. *La Fontaine et le premier recueil des "Fables,"* I, 219.

24. "Irony in La Fontaine: From Message to Massage," p. 86.

25. "Four Modes of Double Irony in La Fontaine's *Fables,*" p. 206.

26. *La Fontaine: Fables,* p. 40.

27. J. Dubois and R. Lagane, *Dictionnaire de la langue française classique*, 2nd ed. (Paris: Librairie Classique Eugène Belin, 1960), p. 137.

28. *La Fontaine fabuliste*, p. 96.

29. *La Fontaine et le premier recueil des "Fables,"* II, 207.

30. I am grateful to Professor J. Max Patrick, whose criticism of an early draft of my remarks on this poem helped to sharpen my analysis of the satyr's reaction; much of the discussion included here appeared as an article entitled, "Selection and Sacrifice in La Fontaine's 'Le Satyre et le passant,' " *Papers on French Seventeenth Century Literature*, No. 8 (Winter 1977–78), pp. 196–207.

31. For a valuable discussion of the two fundamental perspectives opposed in this poem, "la vision réaliste et comique" and "la vision poétique et lyrique," see Jacques-Henri Périvier's article " 'La Cigale et la fourmi' comme introduction aux *Fables*," *French Review*, 42 (1969), 418–27.

32. *Fable's End: Completeness and Closure in Rhetorical Fiction* (Chicago: Univ. of Chicago Press, 1974), pp. 14–16.

33. "The Art of Allegory in La Fontaine's *Fables*," *French Review*, 45 (1972), 1130.

IV

Irony and Texture

What I will be calling texture in La Fontaine's poetry derives from a long-standing distinction between texture and structure traceable to John Crowe Ransom and the American "New Critics": whereas structure is "the explicit argument or paraphrasable statement made in a poem," texture is considered to be "everything else—the phonetic pattern, the sequence of images, the meanings suggested by the connotations of words, etc."[1] Separating these concepts during the act of explication will not always be a simple matter, but acknowledging their difference can be helpful in explaining the foundations of La Fontaine's literary art. Although every word in the *Fables* must remain in a sense discursive, by virtue of the ineradicable denotative properties of language, the poet consistently moves beyond simple, direct communication by endowing his vocabulary with what Brody calls "semantic surplus." This linguistic residue, while underscoring La Fontaine's awareness that poetic language is qualitatively distinguishable from other kinds, holds many secrets to the mechanics of his ironic imagination.

When the oak says to the reed, "Tout vous est Aquilon, tout me semble Zéphir" (in "Le Chêne et le roseau," I, 22), he is delivering an explicit—though misplaced—message. But what he says (the structural surface of banal interlocution) is far less interesting than the catalytic reciprocity exercised by the words of this alexandrine and by the other words in their poetic surroundings. *Aquilon,* cold and violent, is alleged to be an attribute of the fragile reed; *Zéphir,* soft and gentle, *seems* to be the oak's per-

sonal wind. But rhyme conspires to heighten the tenta-
tiveness of *semble*, because the echoing *souffrir* shades the
appearance of *Zéphir* with the reality of an imminent
uprooting. The one whose prideful summit now "Brave
l'effort de la tempête," confidently unaware of his tenuous hold on the soil, will soon discover that both poles of
his antithetical boast have been negated: *Tout ne vous est
point Aquilon, tout ne me semble plus Zéphir*. The level of
deceiving appearance having been literally torn down,
the ironist can dwell in peace, with reader and reed, on
the sturdy ground of better understanding as soon as a
formidable north wind ". . . déracine / Celui de qui la tête
au Ciel était voisine, / Et dont les pieds touchaient à l'Empire des Morts."

The ironic texture of "Le Lion et le moucheron" (II, 9)
assumes a variety of humorous forms. The fable opens
with an alexandrine that scholars have long recognized as
a parody of a line by Malherbe directed against Concini,
maréchal d'Ancre ("Va-t'en à la malheure, excrément de la
terre"):

> Va-t'en, chétif insecte, excrément de la terre.
> C'est en ces mots que le Lion
> Parlait un jour au Moucheron.

The lion's harsh denunciation of the gnat is doubly undermined: the inflated style in which the insult is uttered
contrasts pointedly with the size of the foe being at-
tacked, while the physical disparity opposing the adversaries is reduced phonetically (the homophonic *-on* at the
end of lines two and three comically unites the characters)
and even reversed when the length of each vocable is
considered (letter and syllable counts favor the *Moucheron*
rather than the *Lion*). But a retrospective analysis of the
poem will confirm that the ironist is aiming here in both
directions at once: his barbs will strike the tiny winged
creature as well as the haughty carnivore. As for the gnat,

he parries the logic of the epithet *chétif* by declaring war on the lion and by mocking his implicit claims of superiority: "Un boeuf est plus puissant que toi, / Je le mène à ma fantaisie." Heedless of the lion's "titre de Roi" which might intimidate others, the gnat ". . . sonna la charge, / Fut le Trompette et le Héros." The elevation of this incident through the use of mock-heroic language signals an ironic tension indicative of what Booth calls "clashes of style":

> If a speaker's style departs notably from whatever the reader considers the normal way of saying a thing, or the way normal for this speaker, the reader may suspect irony. (*A Rhetoric of Irony*, p. 67)

The speaker here is the ("heterodiegetic") narrator but the lofty attitude being transmitted is that of the gnat, who views his impending battle in epic terms. The reader's norm excludes bombast from the range of acceptable ways to describe an incident of minimal consequence. Our knowledge of La Fontaine's fondness for adopting an incongruous tone (for example, the very next fable begins in this manner: "Un Anier, son Sceptre à la main, / Menait, en Empereur Romain, / Deux Coursiers à longues oreilles") helps to situate his *Trompette* and *Héros* in their discordant context. The attack itself is introduced in a similar vein:

> Dans l'abord il se met au large,
> Puis prend son temps, fond sur le cou
> Du Lion, qu'il rend presque fou.

The mock-ritualistic tonality of the scene is undercut by the line-ending assonance of *cou* and *fou*. The aggressor's presence is devalued by pronominal references (*il se met, il rend*), whereas the object of hostility stands in nominal prominence as a *rejet* fulfilling the promise of a run-on line. Yet the lion is no less foolish than the gnat:

Le quadrupède écume, et son oeil étincelle;
Il rugit, on se cache, on tremble à l'environ;
     Et cette alarme universelle
     Est l'ouvrage d'un Moucheron.

Commenting on the first noun in the above passage, Jean Dominique Biard contends:

> The graphic evocation of the lion's agitation in his attempt to rid himself of the fly and the contrast between his size and that of his enemy, between the formidable deployment of his ineffective means of defence and the mobility of the fly are increased by the choice of the word *quadrupède*.[2]

Though the lion is equipped with four feet that are doubtless well suited to covering a lot of ground quickly, instead of fleeing he tries to ward off his enemy by glaring and roaring ineffectually. The hyperbolic notion that the gnat's offensive has caused an "alarme universelle" serves as a reminder that the ironist/narrator is in the background contemplating an absurdly impossible situation.

As the description of the battle is elaborated, the tone remains humorous:

Un avorton de Mouche en cent lieux le harcelle,
Tantôt pique l'échine, et tantôt le museau,
     Tantôt entre au fond du naseau,
La rage alors se trouve à son faîte montée.

While enjoying success against the lion, the gnat experiences the setback of finding himself in a separate struggle, grammatical and semantic, that has seen him go from noun to pronoun and back again, and now to a disparaging nominal phrase, "avorton de Mouche." The attacker may be a runt, but he knows how to fight a much bigger opponent. Thus one character is being chided for his puniness, the other for his useless physical advantage. The anaphoric *tantôt*, appearing three times in fourteen syllables, underscores the frenetic but effective activity of the gnat, while the rhyme of *museau* and *naseau* helps to preserve the antiepic aura of the episode by insisting phonetically on its inherently comic basis. However, the elevated phrase, "à son faîte montée," plays a role in keeping alive the tension between expressive levels indicated above in references to *Trompette* and *Héros*.

As the pervasive biting continues, the harassed lion becomes for himself a second formidable enemy:

> L'invisible ennemi triomphe, et rit de voir
> Qu'il n'est griffe ni dent en la bête irritée
> Qui de la mettre en sang ne fasse son devoir.
> Le malheureux Lion se déchire lui-même,
> Fait résonner sa queue à l'entour de ses flancs,
> Bat l'air, qui n'en peut mais; et sa fureur extrême
> Le fatigue, l'abat; le voilà sur les dents.

Overwhelmed by the gnat, the lion is also suffering on the level of connotation: the grace and dignity of *Lion* and *titre de Roi* (even then undercut by the "chétif insecte") had been replaced by the unprepossessing anatomical term *quadrupède*, which in turn gives way to an even more deflated word, *bête*. And the nominal *bête* assumes adjectival qualities as teeth and claws inflict pain on their possessor. Whereas the lion's head is of no help in freeing him from difficulty, his failure to *raisonner* is comically compensated by the nearly homophonous *résonner*, as in his discomfort the lion wildly wags his opposite extremity. The interplay of *Bat* and *abat* emphasizes the hopelessness of his predicament: in his efforts to defend himself he thrashes nothing but air, and it is ultimately his own empty wrath that wears him down. Exhausted by the confrontation ("On dit . . . qu'on est *sur les dents*, que le grand travail a mis quelqu'un sur les dents, pour dire qu'il est las et fatigué, qu'il n'en peut plus": Furetière, quoted by Couton in *F*, p. 421, n. 6), the lion is also *sur les dents* in a literal sense: his dental weapons, ineffectual against an "invisible ennemi," have damaged only his own flesh.

But the gnat is confidently unaware that his triumph is to be strikingly short-lived:

> L'insecte du combat se retire avec gloire:
> Comme il sonna la charge, il sonne la victoire,
> Va partout l'annoncer, et rencontre en chemin
>   L'embuscade d'une araignée:
>   Il y rencontre aussi sa fin.

Despite the mock-heroic flavor of the passage, by calling his victorious warrior an *insecte* the author adds another indicator that his winged protagonist is hardly Homeric. Given the context, the inversion of *se retire du combat* acquires a funny resonance, as does the rhymed pairing of *gloire* and *victoire*, terms that are made to descend rapidly the path leading from the summit of success to the valley of entrapment (the gnat's *chemin* takes him inexorably, phonetically, to his *fin*). The *araignée*, placed in rhyming position, points vocally to the first line of the five-verse double moral ("Quelle chose par là nous peut être enseignée?"), but the spider's lesson, like her web, hangs well enough without external support. The reversal accomplished by the ambush has come close to confirming the lion's abusive description of the gnat as "excrément de la terre," the quasi-noble *fils de l'air* (cf. the fly's prideful description of herself as "la fille de l'air" in "La Mouche et la fourmi," IV, 3) having become in his immobility nothing more than a factor in the spider's digestive processes.

"La Grenouille et le rat" (IV, 11), a fable that focuses on a somewhat analogous reversal, opens with a proverb cast in archaic language: "Tel, comme dit Merlin, cuide

engeigner autrui, / Qui souvent s'engeigne soi-même"
(glossed by Couton as "Tel croit monter un piège pour
autrui, qui souvent s'y prend lui-même": *F*, p. 441, n. 2).
In this poem a frog finds appetizing a certain rat "qui ne
connaissait l'Avent ni le Carême"; as Biard points out,
this "religious reference . . . applied to the fat rat together
with the title of *Messire*, given to clerics, evokes the ro-
tund monkish figure of the *gaulois* tradition" (p. 112). As
is so often the case in the *Fables*, here the animal and
human levels intersect in a counterpoint of spirited irony.
What the rat is promised is what he will become—if
everything proceeds according to plan ("je vous ferai fes-
tin," says the frog to entice her intended victim). Both
levels remain intact when the scene shifts to the marsh
that the frog calls home:

> Dans le marais entrés, notre bonne commère
> S'efforce de tirer son hôte au fond de l'eau,
> Contre le droit des gens, contre la foi jurée;
> Prétend qu'elle en fera gorge-chaude et curée;
> (C'était, à son avis, un excellent morceau.)

This *commère* (from the ecclesiastical Latin term *commater*,
meaning "mère avec": *NDE*, p. 181) is neither a *marraine*
nor, more broadly, a *voisine* in any positive sense: she will
show her hospitality by feasting on the guest. The legalis-
tic phrases, "le droit des gens" and "la foi jurée," function like the "foi d'animal" of I, 1, for instance, by sound-
ing notes evocative of human jurisprudence against an
animal (in this case amphibian) descant. The terms *gorge-
chaude* and *curée* define the rat as hunter's game while
tacitly comparing the frog to a bird of prey (and also, in
the second case, possibly to a hunting dog).[3] The link,
through assonance, of *eau* and *morceau* couples place and
event by suggesting where the banquet will be held. Yet
another image of food consumption is advanced in the

next verse as the frog thinks about the anticipated repast: "Déjà dans son esprit la galande le croque." But this reverie of happy munching will be no more than a dream; as the frog struggles with the rat,

> Un Milan qui dans l'air planait, faisait la ronde,
> Voit d'en haut le pauvret se débattant sur l'onde.
> Il fond dessus, l'enlève, et, par même moyen
>   La Grenouille et le lien.
>   Tout en fut; tant et si bien,
>   Que de cette double proie
>   L'oiseau se donne au coeur joie,
>   Ayant de cette façon
>   A souper chair et poisson.

The kite's two-for-the-price-of-one abduction does, of course, illustrate the introductory aphorism ("Tel ... cuide engeigner autrui ..."), so the event itself holds no surprise for the reader; on the other hand, the manner of the telling (the narrative texture) rescues the scene from being lifelessly predictable. The large bird concretizes the activity of the ironizing author, who hovers in amusement, pen in hand, above his hapless victims. The appearance of tenderness (the rat is depicted as *le pauvret*, but from whose perspective—the bird's or the narrator's?) is erased by the reality of rapaciousness as the winged predator foils the hungry frog's dining plans. All pleasant notions of togetherness implied by the noun *lien (couple, rapport, liaison, affinité,* and so on) are vitiated in this atmosphere of brute survival. But the episode is not being painted in tragic hues; the pairing of *proie* and *joie* suggests that feelings of pain and pleasure depend, as everybody knows, on the angle of vision (or of taste): from this bird's point of view, "Messire Rat" and the scheming frog are no more than his mealtime fish and meat.

The story has been told, its presumed import animatedly dramatized. Thus the heptasyllabic quatrain with which La Fontaine concludes the poem will possibly seem superfluous:

> La ruse la mieux ourdie
> Peut nuire à son inventeur;
> Et souvent la perfidie
> Retourne sur son auteur.

But does the moral explicitness of the opening verses necessarily become, in the final four lines, redundantly overt? The irony of "La Grenouille et le rat" is no doubt local, and until now it has appeared to be quite stable (and open from the outset): the frog has joined the parade of losers in the *trompeur trompé* syndrome (though the rat, unlike the rooster in "Le Coq et le renard," II, 15, does not experience the satisfaction of turning the tables). It might be argued, however, that the ending of this fable adds an element of covert instability. The possible increase of interpretive options is caused by language producing what Booth calls "conflicts of belief":

> ... we are alerted whenever we notice an unmistakable conflict between the beliefs expressed and the beliefs we hold *and suspect the author of holding*. We can see the resulting ironies most clearly when there is an incredible passage in the midst of straightforward writing. (p. 73)

The words *ruse* and *perfidie* can be applied to the frog's trickery, to be sure, but the second term seems unusually severe in the circumstances (*perfide* echoes its Latin source, *perfidus*—"qui viole sa foi": NDE, p. 552). The poet had taken care to draw an amusing portrait of the frog, so that the abrupt shift from light-heartedness to sobriety has a suspicious ring. Is the narrator really judging the frog as perfidious? If so, why is her stratagem punished while the kite, who had the same objective in view, escapes retribution? Is one of these characters more reprehensible than the other? In this context the modal verb seems particularly significant: "La ruse la mieux ourdie / *Peut* nuire . . ." (but not inevitably). And it is pertinent to note that the poet has chosen the adverb *souvent* instead of *toujours:* life is complex enough to admit exceptions to virtually every rule (as the *Fables* abundantly attest). Or the fabulist may be suggesting that he has terminated the anecdote at a convenient (but not absolute) stopping point, and that in a subsequent episode the kite could easily fall victim himself to a superior opponent. In any event, the supposed lesson of the fable is less fixed than it appears, and the texture of the narration is out of harmony with the tone of the aphoristic parentheses.

That the treacherous do not unavoidably become victims is made clear in "Les Poissons et le cormoran" (X, 3), another poem in which the ironic texture overshadows the ostensible subject. Like "L'Homme et la couleuvre" (X, 1), to be discussed at length in the next chapter, the fable about the fish and the cormorant deals with the manifestations of a power structure:

> Il n'était point d'étang dans tout le voisinage
> Qu'un Cormoran n'eût mis à contribution.
> Viviers et réservoirs lui payaient pension.

Unlike the man in the first fable of Book X, however, this ravenous cormorant has begun to feel the debilitating effects of old age. This condition might well have disastrous consequences, as the poet indicates, because "Tout Cormoran se sert de pourvoyeur lui-même." This declaration recasts in a wryly grim perspective the three lines just quoted. The seabird's *voisinage* does not convey a sense of neighborhood; it is merely the precinct where he goes shopping for food. He makes use of whatever he finds there for his mealtime pleasure (the noun in *mettre à contribution*—literally *to make use of*—refers by implication to a tax of flesh). What he was accustomed to receiving from fish-ponds and reservoirs was really a *pension* (meaning *payment for board):* unlike the amusing hoarder in the following poem ("L'Enfouisseur et son compère"), he would readily dispense with his collected fees by eating them. The snake's indictment of the powerful man in fable 1 could apply equally well to the cormorant: ". . . ta justice, / C'est ton utilité, ton plaisir, ton caprice," for the universe exists as a function of his needs.

Whereas the mindless turtle in fable 2 ("La Tortue et les deux canards") had been blinded by conceit, the cormorant owes his diminished sight to elderliness (he was "un peu trop vieux pour voir au fond des eaux"), yet he proves better equipped to cope with his physical ailment than the slow-witted turtle could handle her ego-based infirmity. How does the bird confront his "disette extrême"? Necessity once again gives birth to invention:

> Que fit-il? Le besoin, docteur en stratagème,
> Lui fournit celui-ci. Sur le bord d'un Etang
>   Cormoran vit une Ecrevisse.
> Ma commère, dit-il, allez tout à l'instant
>   Porter un avis important
>   A ce peuple. Il faut qu'il périsse:
> Le maître de ce lieu dans huit jours pêchera.

The dramatic irony of the scene is evident. We know that the crayfish will be the cormorant's ally only insofar as she serves his gluttonous purposes, but the form of address he chooses, "Ma commère," gives the illusion of equality. The "avis important" to which he refers will indeed have life-and-death significance for his intended victims, the fish in the vicinity ("ce peuple"), but not precisely in the way he will have the message presented (as the words of the crayfish are to be construed, their true meaning will be masked). The rhyming pair *Ecrevisse* and *périsse* only partly conceals the reality of her mission: she will be enlisted as an agent of death.

Her words are not taken lightly: "L'Ecrevisse en hâte s'en va / Conter le cas: grande est l'émute." In this poem the crayfish is virtually nothing but a mouthpiece. She does the bird's bidding without posing a single question; in no way does she lead us to believe she is aware that her announcement will serve to set a deadly trap. The role she plays in this poem is very different from that accorded her crustacean model in La Fontaine's source, Pilpay.[4] La Fontaine, by strictly subordinating her once aggressive function, clearly gives primacy to the cormorant's actions. Whereas he delights elsewhere in showing how the deceiver is deceived (as we have seen), here he is content to explore the effects of unchecked trickery.

At this point in the narrative, we still do not know whether the cormorant's plan will be successfully carried out. Will the fish be devoured or will they manage to evade annihilation? Suspense there may be, but not real concern. La Fontaine's language, even in the service of subjects that have tragic potential, will continually thwart any urge to react, as we read the *Fables*, in the manner that we might understandably react to events in *Hamlet* or *Madame Bovary*. The alarmed fish may be rushing toward swift destruction, but in describing their *émute* (possibly a dialectal form, theorizes Couton: *F*, p. 519, n. 3) the poet carefully avoids creating tragic or otherwise solemn overtones:

> On court, on s'assemble, on députe
> A l'Oiseau: Seigneur Cormoran,
> D'où vous vient cet avis? Quel est votre garand?
> Etes-vous sûr de cette affaire?
> N'y savez-vous remède? Et qu'est-il bon de faire?

How does La Fontaine assure the comic impact of the passage? That the potential victims are fish rather than humans may influence the reader's response, but La Fontaine can present even the death of human characters in a funny light (as was pointed out in the earlier discussion of "La Jeune Veuve" and "Le Curé et le mort"). Further-more, all the personages in the *Fables* function on the same ontological plane, so that the death of one is neither more nor less actual, in extraliterary terms, than that of another character. It is the tone of the passage that guar-antees our amused reaction. The writer packs three present-tense action verbs—"On court, on s'assemble, on députe"—in a single octosyllable. In each case the subject is the impersonal *on:* the reader will have difficulty identi-fying with nameless, faceless characters—whether they be fish, fowl, or Frenchmen. The cormorant's aquatic neighbors are sending delegates to confer with their "Seigneur": inadvertently, perhaps, they are calling at-tention to his advanced age, which had threatened to ren-der him innocuous (the etymological connection, *plus âgé,* is apposite here: see *NDE,* p. 681); and this term, ostensi-bly a respectful form, serves in this context to parody feu-dal relationships; elsewhere the phrases "Seigneur Ours" (V, 20) and "Seigneur Loup" (VIII, 17) play similar roles. The substantive *garand* reinforces the juridical allure of the dialogue.

How should the water-dwelling delegates counter the impending threat? "Changer de lieu," says the cormo-rant, capitalizing on their confusion. When the stymied fish ask how this might be done, the bird is reassuring:

> —N'en soyez point en soin: je vous porterai tous,
>   L'un après l'autre, en ma retraite.
> Nul que Dieu seul et moi n'en connaît les chemins:
>   Il n'est demeure plus secrète.
> Un Vivier que nature y creusa de ses mains,
>   Inconnu des traîtres humains,
>   Sauvera votre république.

The situation unfolding here is somewhat analogous to that of the turtle and ducks of fable 2. What appear to be the main differences and similarities in the two sets of circumstances? In both cases a journey is proposed; those to whom travel is offered seemingly stand to benefit from the voyage, but in the end they die. There are likewise a number of significant contrasts: the turtle abandons the security of her hole to venture widely (like the ill-fated rat of Book VIII who becomes an oyster's lunch), but the fish will leave the freedom of their pond (their liberty now seemingly menaced) in order to enter the cormorant's reportedly safe, but actually dangerous, den; this bird has a vested interest in the acceptance of his proposal, whereas the ducks are—in a double sense—the vehicles of the narrator's ironic storytelling, and they do not profit from the turtle's flamboyant fall; finally, a single journey in fable 2 is replaced, in fable 3, by a series of identical trips in no way particularized (thus we see that the fish exist simply as a means of satisfying the bird's appetite). This merging and diverging of structural elements lends weight to the view (to be developed in chapter V) that the arrangement of fables in books, whatever may have motivated the decision, was no arbitrary act.

The figure of the labyrinth, an apparent organizing principle in Book X (as will be shown), is dominant in the passage under discussion. The fish are unable to venture alone through the tangle separating them from ostensible safety; they must rely on the assumption (as they will discover) that the cormorant's offer of help is honorable. He will carry each of them along the pathways of his maze to a most promising destination: a *Vivier* (a fish-preserve or breeding-ground, where they will presumably be protected, grow healthily plump, and procreate). But the cormorant's design mocks the Latin origin of *Vivier*; the noun *vivarium*, from the verb *vivere* (to live), denotes an "endroit où l'on garde des animaux vivants" (*NDE*, p. 796)—yet the fish of this fable will remain alive only until the cormorant elects to put them on his menu. Deprived of the webwork weaponry of his prime ("N'ayant ni filets ni réseaux"), the aging bird will press into service his retirement home ("ma retraite") as a means of practicing his favorite occupation. The privacy of his abode ("Il n'est demeure plus secrète") is a projection of the cormorant's hidden intentions. Whereas the turtle had embarked on a long journey in order to observe "mainte République," the fish of this poem will undertake a short trip for the apparent purpose of saving their tiny republic. In each case, the travelers would have been wise to stay at home.

Predictably, these fish do not manage to unmask the seabird's treachery:

> On le crut. Le peuple aquatique
> L'un après l'autre fut porté
> Sous ce rocher peu fréquenté.
> Là Cormoran le bon apôtre,
> Les ayant mis en un endroit
> Transparent, peu creux, fort étroit,
> Vous les prenait sans peine, un jour l'un, un jour l'autre.

La Fontaine enhances the humor of the episode by fusing human and animal planes via the expressions "peuple aquatique"[5] and "bon apôtre." The latter is a splendid use of antiphrasis: according to most human perspectives, the cormorant is neither good in any conventional sense nor apostolic (the gospel of terror he has deliberately spread bears little resemblance to agape). This adjective-noun combination, which appears several times in the *Contes*, occurs in one other context in the *Fables* (in "Le Chat, la belette, et le petit lapin," VII, 15), its environment revealing even more clearly the ironic thrust of the expression:

> Grippeminaud le bon apôtre
> Jetant des deux côtés la griffe en même temps,
> Mit les plaideurs d'accord en croquant l'un et l'autre.

This figurative usage of *apôtre*, dating from the seventeenth century, is likewise found in Molière, Racine, and

La Bruyère. The activity of the historical apostle, whose vocation is to disseminate spiritual nourishment, is doubly perverted by the cormorant, who draws the fish into his den (the expansiveness of evangelism being replaced by the shrinking of territory—and thus of options for survival —available to the fish) and who claims all sustenance for himself. The poet's triple use of *l'un* and *l'autre* cleverly demonstrates the tension between what the bird says and what he really means: first he promises to bear the fish, one after the other, to his dwelling; then he makes good this pledge; but finally his guests receive attention individually not as the beneficiaries of the good will of waterfowl but as the prey of the web-footed apostle, who proceeds to eat them one by one ("un jour l'un, un jour l'autre"). His description of the preserve ("Un Vivier que nature y creusa de ses mains") had suggested great depth, but his words have effectively tricked the fish, for his hideaway is, most conveniently, "Transparent, peu creux, fort étroit": escape to a low level too dark for his weakening vision is obviously impossible.

What lesson, in the narrator's opinion, has the cormorant succeeded in giving the fish?

> Il leur apprit à leurs dépens
> Que l'on ne doit jamais avoir de confiance
> En ceux qui sont mangeurs de gens.

The last phrase, a bizarre permutation of Jesus' words, "Suivez-moi, et je vous ferai pêcheurs d'hommes" (*Matthew*, 4:19), preserves the mock-biblical flavor of the poem. As for the fish, in a world governed by survival-of-the-hungriest they were doomed in any event:

> Ils y perdirent peu, puisque l'humaine engeance
> En aurait aussi bien croqué sa bonne part;
> Qu'importe qui vous mange? homme ou loup; toute panse

Me paraît une à cet égard;
Un jour plus tôt, un jour plus tard,
Ce n'est pas grande différence.

Lest the reader dwell too long on the potentially saddening import of the events being recounted, the fabulist concludes with a volley of comic terms: *engeance, croqué,* and *panse.* If, as has been suggested, *engeance* is related to an Old French verb meaning *accroître* or *faire pulluler* (see *Petit Robert),* this pejorative word for *race* fits comfortably in a poem concerned with one kind of gluttony; the rhyme of *engeance* with *panse* further stimulates a covert comparison with Messer Gaster, and the verb *croquer* adds mouth to stomach as the two most important parts of the voracious individual's anatomy.

It may be instructive to take a closer look at the narrator's assertion, "Qu'importe qui vous mange? homme ou loup; toute panse / Me paraît une à cet égard": this blurring of ontological distinctions (albeit in a narrow context), coupled with the depreciatory "humaine engeance," would seem to reflect La Fontaine's tendency to free himself (at least as narrative persona) of uncompromising anthropocentric viewpoints. Following the appearance of the 1668 collection of *Fables* (Books I–VI), "La Fontaine tended more and more," as Philip A. Wadsworth has pointed out, "to dignify animals and to undermine the dignity of man."[6] Our awareness of the rich ironic texture of the *Fables* can often be enriched if we remain aware that the perspective underlying the poetry is a kind of zoological democracy. My reading of "Les Compagnons d'Ulysse" (XII, 1) is informed by this assumption.[7]

At the risk of belaboring the self-evident, I would like to lay the groundwork for my analysis of "Les Compagnons d'Ulysse" by discussing briefly the nonreferential nature of literary language. Most would agree that when words appear in an imaginative work they assume functions that are different from those they have when employed for purposes of scientific, journalistic, or everyday communication. Many critics are careful to preserve this distinction, which I. A. Richards expressed concisely several decades ago:

> A statement may be used for the sake of the *reference*, true or false, which it causes. This is the *scientific* use of language. But it may also be used for the sake of the effects in emotion and attitude produced by the reference it occasions. This is the *emotive* use of language.[8]

Leaving aside the thorny issue of affectivity, one may appropriately substitute for *emotive* the term *literary* (or even *poetic*—in a broadly generic sense). This binary classification of linguistic roles, which some would label modish or dismiss as irrelevant, is the explicator's proper starting point, in the classroom as well as in scholarly forums. Wellek and Warren's classic explanation of the closed-circuit reality of literature continues to be a helpful reminder of this basic distinction:

> The [literary] work of art ... appears as an object of knowledge *sui generis* which has a special ontological status. It is neither real (physical, like a statue) nor mental (psychological, like the experience of light or pain) nor ideal (like a triangle). It is a system of norms of ideal concepts which are intersubjective. They must be assumed to exist in collective ideology, changing with it, accessible only through individual mental experiences, based on the sound-structure of its sentences.[9]

Applied to the *Fables*, the principle of verbal dichotomy compels the reader to acknowledge that all of La Fontaine's characters (whether he presents them as humans or beasts, plants or pots) are linguistic phenomena with no existential referent beyond the text where they reside. Dwellers in a verbal domain, they are neither more nor less than the sum of attributes the fabulist has assigned to them in an act of poetic creation. The poet's universe is animated by words such as *cigale, ours, perroquet,* and *singe,* terms likewise used by the naturalist, but these strictly phonological parallels do not make La Fontaine's creatures actual outside their literary frame of reference. By the same token, characters in the *Fables* who are portrayed as human beings have more in common with the reed and the oak than with any of us, operating as they do within a tight esthetic boundary. Thus we are obliged, in each analysis of the *Fables,* to consider the personages in any poem on their own terms (by discovering how they function in their special rarefied environment). Clearly, however, such a procedure does not free the text of extraliterary semantic weight. In other words, La Fontaine's insects, for example, while being poor subject matter for entomological research, are linked by analogy (as opposed to identity) with insects of the zoology lab, so that the explicator's assessment of their behavior in poetic surroundings will be somewhat conditioned by dictionary meanings of *ant* or *cicada* or *fly.* Otherwise, part of the comic impulse of the *Fables* would be lost. For, as we know, a vital element of La Fontaine's humor-making is his skill in playfully foiling, by means of a whole spectrum of ironic strategies, the reader's real-world expectations. The language of the poet constantly alludes to situations, events, and objects within our mental and sensory grasp, but his fables unfold in a realm forever beyond the frontiers of time, space, and matter; his characters thus operate in accordance with laws that are foreign to our experience. La Fontaine's talking animals, as well as his other characters, occupy the same ontological plane as Phèdre and Rastignac.

Since, by its very nature, literature confers ontological equality upon all its citizens, we must avoid approaching the *Fables* with an anthropocentric bias. All the members of La Fontaine's motley cast of performers—men and monkeys and mice—have been created equal: their actions, rather than biology or birthright, determine whether they are to be judged superior or inferior to each other. As for La Fontaine the narrator, he enters the invented world of the *Fables* with an unprejudiced outlook. Whatever may have been his private thoughts about the relative merits of real people and beasts in and around Château-Thierry, the poet is never anthropocentric in his authorial stance. He gaily introduces a host of creatures whose conduct in no way corresponds to a scientifically based hierarchy of intelligent entities. When he deals with the theme of friendship, for instance, birds (in "Les Deux Pigeons," IX, 2) can illustrate the topic as effectively as humans (in "Les Deux Amis," VIII, 11).

Regardless of the subject being treated, we must not interpret literally La Fontaine's allusions to organisms found in the physical world. In reading such lines as "L'Aigle et le Chat-huant leurs querelles cessèrent, / Et firent tant qu'ils s'embrassèrent" (V, 18), we need to bear in mind that the vocables *Aigle* and *Chat-huant* have metaphorical, not organic, value: the fabulist is telling us, in effect, that we are to imagine a pair of linguistic entities possessing, respectively, the attributes of *eagle* and *owl*. In their happy complicity, author and reader are both fully aware that the poem has nothing to do with ornithology. When La Fontaine writes, "Je me sers d'Animaux pour instruire les Hommes" (in the epistle "A Monseigneur le Dauphin," introducing Book I), he is not referring to the pedagogical talents of flesh-and-blood animals. Nor is that his meaning at the end of his career when he declares, "Les Animaux sont les précepteurs des Hommes dans mon ouvrage" (in the dedicatory letter to the Duc de Bourgogne preceding the poems of Book XII). He did not even have to draw on his background as *maître des eaux et forêts* in order to recognize that his wonderful menagerie differed radically from all the animals he had ever encountered outside his imagination. What is significant about La Fontaine's assertions that he uses animals to teach men is that he admits his nonhuman characters without discrimination into the universe of the *Fables*.

In short, these fictional animals, divorced from empirical reality, have absolute *droit de cité* in La Fontaine's fantasy world. It is especially important to remember this point when one studies "Les Compagnons d'Ulysse," the opening poem of the final book of *Fables*, published in 1694 (Book XII in modern editions). This is a poem whose import eludes easy resolution because of the tension between the poet/narrator's ostensible attitude toward his material and the internal thrust of the anecdote itself. The discord between La Fontaine's introductory and closing remarks, on one hand, and the thematic movement of the central episode, on the other, is an anomaly stemming, it would appear, from the author's awkwardness in addressing two audiences simultaneously. Like other fables in this and the first eleven books, "Les Compagnons d'Ulysse" raises issues aimed principally at adult readers; yet the poem is dedicated to the king's grandson, the Duc de Bourgogne, who was just eight years old when the fable first appeared in the *Mercure Galant* in December 1690. After a prefatory section in which he obligingly flatters the young prince ("l'unique objet du soin des Immortels"), the fabulist announces the poem's real subject and his presumed judgment of it: he will tell of an incident in which the Greeks,

> Imprudents et peu circonspects,
> S'abandonnèrent à des charmes
> Qui métamorphosaient en bêtes les humains.

Then, following the main eighty-line passage describing the metamorphosis of Ulysses' companions and the viewpoint of three of them toward their new existence, the poet condemns them for letting their passions reign. Speaking again directly to the young prince, he concludes the fable by saying of the transformed compagnons:

> Ils ont force pareils en ce bas Univers:
> Gens à qui j'impose pour peine
> Votre censure et votre haine.

Although the fable seems to attain a high degree of formal closure, thematic resolution is not achieved. Philip A. Wadsworth has plausibly argued that "le prologue et l'épilogue . . . trahissent une certaine gêne" produced by the poet's need to tailor his topic to the royal child's edification.[10] Similarly, David Lee Rubin has commented on these three verses by maintaining: "Like the convoluted and unctuous overture in praise of the duke, this harsh and mean-spirited finale is so uncharacteristic of La Fontaine's tone and thought that it suggests a great gulf between the implied author and the narrator."[11] Evidence to be found in the apologue proper would indeed seem to indicate that the pedagogical emphasis in "Les Compagnons d'Ulysse" is at best a cumbersome restraint working at cross purposes with full artistic development. The most fitting candidate for the impartial reader's amused *censure* is Ulysses, who "is far from being a model of rationality" (Rubin, p. 209) and who proves to be no match for the articulate beasts whose new life is incomparably nicer than their former state.

The story told in this poem arrestingly corroborates La Fontaine's famous declaration, "Mon imitation n'est point un esclavage" (*OD,* p. 648). He offers here a selective and original development of the metamorphosis, by Circé, of Ulysses' traveling companions, an episode inspired by Homer's *Odyssey.*[12] Significantly, the French poet indicates that the human existence of these characters had been quite unpleasant: "Les Compagnons d'Ulysse, après dix ans d'alarmes, / Erraient au gré du vent, de leur sort incertains." Here, at the outset, is conveyed an image of men lacking self-determination, men whose destiny is controlled by the wind. After arriving at Circé's court, all the travelers except Ulysses are transformed into animals, big and small, under the influence of a powerful concoction Circé gives them ("un breuvage / Délicieux, mais plein d'un funeste poison"). Having persuaded the nymph to return his friends to their former condition, Ulysses approaches three of them in turn—a lion, a bear, and a wolf—to spread the presumably good news that they need not remain beasts. Before he embarks on this mission, the sorceress hints that a major struggle may be in store: "Il obtint qu'on rendrait à ces Grecs leur figure. / Mais la voudront-ils bien, dit la Nymphe, accepter?" More prophetic words were never spoken. For Jean Dominique Biard, the reference to "*ces* Grecs" has a humorous quality: "The demonstrative points to a motley collection of animals into which Ulysses' companions have been metamorphosed and stresses the comic discrepancy between their appearance and their human nature."[13] But the nature of these characters, after their magical transformation, is no longer human. They are neither anthropomorphous nor psychologically anthropic. From their point of view the *breuvage* of the sorceress has had only beneficial effects.

Does the lion wish to become human again? "Je n'ai pas la tête si folle," he candidly replies. So immersed is he in his lionhood that he is even unaware of the miraculous restoration of human speech ("On vous rend déjà la parole," Ulysses had promised); as he speaks, the lion imagines himself roaring. No longer a mere soldier or a modest citizen of Ithaca, he is now a king whose teeth and claws are ideal for self-defense. (Absent, implicitly, is the stereotypical leonine aggressiveness, for the line "J'ai griffe et dent, et mets en pièces qui m'attaque" suggests that this lion will gladly fight, but only if pressed.) Without attempting to counter the lion's reasoning, Ulysses proceeds to interview the bear. In Ulysses' opinion, the bear is less attractive in his new form than he had been as a man. To the derisive "Comme te voilà fait!" uttered by his former leader, the bear, with disarming simplicity, opposes these

words: "Comme me voilà fait? comme doit être un ours."
Ulysses is portrayed here as an absolutist who judges the
world from a totally human perspective. But the bear sensi-
bly invokes a modest relativism: "Qui t'a dit qu'une forme
est plus belle qu'une autre? / Est-ce à la tienne à juger de
la nôtre?" Humans may have the right to set standards of
human beauty, but they are not thereby entitled to evalu-
ate the beauty or ugliness of bears. Like the lion, the bear
prefers not to exchange his present condition for human
shape and personality. Why, indeed, should he favor the
uncertain life of a seafarer in contrast to the free, blissful,
untroubled life of a bear? For this is the way he character-
izes his current existence, and Ulysses offers no rebuttal.
Instead, he goes off to talk to the wolf.

Each encounter between man and animal in this poem
is more extensive than the preceding one. This third conversation is longer than the other two combined: it occu-
pies twenty-two lines. Having already been turned down
twice, Ulysses is eager to win at least one convert to the
human race. His tactic this time is to appeal to what may
remain of the wolf's humane instincts. A lovely young
shepherdess, he says, has complained that this very wolf
had been eating her sheep. This report distresses Ulysses,
who recalls that when the wolf was a man he lived honor-
ably and would have saved the fold instead of devouring
it. He begs the wolf to leave the woods and to become
once again an "homme de bien." The wolf begins his
twelve-line reply by wondering whether such men even
exist. The flat dismissal of the topic offered in the original
Mercure Galant version—"Laissons cette matière"—has
been replaced in the 1694 edition by these more vigorous
words: "Pour moi, je n'en vois guère." The wolf, who has
been both man and beast, apparently does not find the
prospect of spending his days as an "homme de bien" at
all compelling (whatever else he may have accomplished
as a man, he endured ten years of torment on the high
seas), and he does not believe that Ulysses, as a representa-

tive of mankind, is justified in indicting him for being a "bête carnassière." In the absence of wolves, people would eat the very sheep whose loss has vexed the village. (The wolf's sudden shift from *tu* to *vous* denotes a deft broadside launched against human gluttony: "N'auriez-vous pas sans moi / Mangé ces animaux que plaint tout le Village?") Similarly, in "Le Loup et les bergers" (X, 5) it is argued that wolves, widely despised for their cruelty, are no more bloodthirsty than men. As for this wolf, he now points out that people perhaps kill each other as readily as they slaughter animals: "Pour un mot quelquefois vous vous étranglez tous," and his next remark—"Ne vous êtes-vous pas l'un à l'autre des Loups?"—comically echoes the formula of the English philosopher Hobbes, *homo homini lupus* (man is a wolf toward man).[14] If carnage prevails in both lupine and human societies, what can possibly be the advantage in abandoning one of these groups for the other?[15] Having considered the option proposed by Ulysses, the wolf claims that ". . . scélérat pour scélérat, / Il vaut mieux être un Loup qu'un Homme." For him there is no question of a toss-up; in a league of scoundrels it is better to be a wolf.[16] And he adds the firm octosyllabic refrain spoken earlier by the lion and then by the bear: "Je ne veux point changer d'état." Ulysses chooses again to remain silent. Not a single word does he utter in refutation of the wolf's logic.

In the next eight lines, which contain no dialogue as such, we learn that Ulysses proceeds to visit his other metamorphosed companions, each of whom rejects his offer to rejoin the human race. (By contrast, their counterparts in Homer's version, having all been changed into swine, are at last restored to their original human form. Here again the Lafontainian principle of "selection and sacrifice" is operative with interesting consequences.) La Fontaine's narrator appears to side, as he does in both introduction and conclusion, with Ulysses against the animals. These creatures are criticized for allowing their appetites to govern them, for spurning the glory (or praise) of noble deeds: "Tous renonçaient au lôs des belles actions." Taken at face value, this assertion seems a colossal case of question-begging: Ulysses has failed to demonstrate that humans in his world act more commendably than beasts. (The heroism and generosity of which real-life people are capable is once again beside the point.) Perhaps, by employing *lôs* (the Pléiade edition gives *lot*), the narrator subtly distances himself from Ulysses' point of view. Whether the term is interpreted to mean *gloire* or *louange*, its use here may succeed in creating a jocular resonance out of keeping with the solemn tone of "belles actions."[17] The writer may be suggesting that the human exploits being rejected by these beasts are neither as glorious as alleged nor as worthy of praise. Yet the ten lines following this statement, which conclude the poem, do not elaborate on the ironic potential of *lôs*. The narrator's assessment of the animals' conduct is harsh: "Ils croyaient s'affranchir suivants leurs passions, / Ils étaient esclaves d'eux-mêmes." It is tempting, in the absence of ironic markers, to read literally this apparently straightforward pronouncement. Fortified by the presumed authorial verdict, Renée Kohn states that Circé's magic spell has succeeded in delivering Ulysses' comrades "à leurs passions maîtresses, leur donnant une illusion de liberté qui ne fait que mieux les asservir à eux-mêmes." As for the ultimate effect of Circé's witchcraft, "Cette prétendue métamorphose transforme les hommes en ce qu'ils sont. Ayant perdu la raison, ils se trouvent entièrement possédés par leurs faiblesses. . . ."[18] But there is nothing demonstrably unreasonable about the thinking processes of these animals. And to contend that they are governed by their weaknesses is likewise a puzzling evaluation of the textual evidence. On the contrary, as Jacques-Henri Périvier argues, the reader "comprend que les compagnons d'Ulysse . . . refusent de redevenir hommes," though Périvier's path to this conclusion seems to be paved with extraliterary concepts of good and evil:

> En faisant d'eux des bêtes, c'est-à-dire en les privant de leur âme spirituelle, la déesse magicienne les a délivrés du mal. . . . Livrés à eux-mêmes, ils jouissent sans scrupule, sans arrière-pensée. Ils satisfont toutes leurs envies sans que les *impedimenta* de la conscience ne viennent entraver leurs plaisirs ou modérer leur faim.[19]

From whatever critical angle the reader may approach this poem, the incident involving Ulysses and his companions illustrates neither the self-deception of the latter nor their blind enslavement to passions. The text does not suggest what ability to reason they might have possessed prior to their transformation (we learn only—in very vague terms—that upon drinking the "liqueur traîtresse" they "perdent la raison," an assertion denied by their perspicacity in dealing with Ulysses). We know little of the quality of their humanness before the encounter with Circé. But we are certain they had a rugged, unrewarding existence. And if we condemn them now, on cue from the narrator, we can do so only with reference to standards of humanness and animality that cease to be pertinent inside the text.[20] For the men transformed into beasts who chant "Je ne veux point changer d'état" certainly know themselves better than do their unfortunate counterparts in so many other fables. These beneficiaries of metamorphosis in "Les Compagnons d'Ulysse," animals in spite of themselves, are understandably satisfied with the gifts that Circé's potion has unexpectedly bestowed on them: for the lion this means authority and strength; for the bear, freedom and tranquillity—"le repos, le repos, trésor si précieux" (as the fabulist exclaims in a different context: VII, 11); for the wolf, there is contentment in the rugged individualism of outlaw and game-hunter. They are all secure in their newfound self-knowledge. It is Ulysses, rather than any of his companions, who plays the "rôle dérisoire" in this little drama, as Wadsworth maintains.[21] The narrator's favorable portrait of the Ithacan leader (". . . il joignait à la sagesse / La mine d'un Héros et le doux entretien") is not borne out when he confronts the three advocates of animal nature. Paradoxically, as Rubin states, "By the narrator's own standard, the duc de Bourgogne should hate Ulysses and admire his companions!" (p. 209). Though the authorial comments framing the main narrative tend to mask its import ("Il fallait sans doute faire des changements de dernière heure, surtout pour ajouter un prologue élogieux et une moralité édifiante qui désavoue les idées cyniques de la fable elle-même": Wadsworth, p. 110), "Les Compagnons d'Ulysse" is thematically related to those fables in which La Fontaine as literary persona suggests that human beings are not necessarily superior to beasts: in "L'Homme et la couleuvre" (X, 1), for instance, when he mentions "l'animal pervers," he quickly adds this wry parenthetical explanation: "C'est le serpent que je veux dire, / Et non l'homme: on pourrait aisément s'y tromper"; and the action of the poem amply justifies calling the man in it (deaf as he is to the reasonable testimony of a cow, an ox, and a tree) an *animal pervers*.

Now such remarks must be placed in perspective. It would be absurd to infer from the *Fables* the judgment that in the real world kings and scholars belong to an order of life no higher than those of snakes and slugs. But this contention is not at all illogical in the internal context of La Fontaine's poetry. The fabulist is not saying, either to the preadolescent prince or to posterity, that people would be better off with a long tail, webbed feet, or gills. Obviously not. But in the self-contained environment of the *Fables*, nonhuman characters are not automatically inferior (either in ability or in performance) to those labeled human. As we have seen, the nonhuman debaters in "Les Compagnons d'Ulysse" are endowed with keen forensic skill. In some other fables in Book XII, animals fare at least as well as humans. The third poem in this final book, "Du Thésauriseur et du singe," focuses on a laughable hoarder who does not realize that fortune stashed away will do him little good. He spends his time frenetically counting his wealth ("Calculant, supputant, comptant comme à la tâche"—actions that might well earn him a place in a Bergsonian casebook on the wellsprings of comedy). His life is complicated by a monkey ("Un gros Singe plus sage, à mon sens, que son maître," states the narrator); the calculation of the treasure's size is constantly rendered incorrect because each time the monkey tosses a gold coin out the window. The poet implies that this playful but perspicacious primate may be at least as capable of knowing pleasure as the human miser. (This notion is echoed by the consonance of *Singe* and *sage.*) In a long poem in the same book (XII, 15), four animals (a crow, a gazelle, a tortoise, and a rat) are being enlisted—claims the narrator —to instruct humans in the meaning of friendship. People are portrayed here as cruel, a dog being called "maudit instrument / Du plaisir barbare des hommes," and a hunter is made to look ridiculous by the clever quartet of beasts. And in another poem (XII, 7), an unlikely trio of characters (a bat, a bush, and a duck) find ingenious ways to avoid their creditors.

Book XII does introduce a few animals that are in no sense models for emulation. For example, a humorous response, not admiration, is evoked by the two stubborn goats (XII, 4) who meet on a narrow bridge, refuse to let each other pass, and as a result fall into the water. A similar source of amusement is the hungry fox (XII, 9) whose nature proves to be stronger than the instruction he receives in wolflike behavior. Another fable (XII, 19) derides the mindless monkey who imitates human wife-beaters. All classes of characters, in short, are eligible targets for the harmless arrows of La Fontaine's wit, just as a swallow is no less likely than an elderly man to be the recipient of the poet's laurels (see "L'Hirondelle et les petits oiseaux," I, 8; "Le Vieillard et les trois jeunes hommes," XI, 8).

Since the world of the *Fables* is autonomous, an objective reading of "Les Compagnons d'Ulysse" can easily draw forth sympathy for the viewpoints of the wolf, bear, and lion, who independently discover that their strange metamorphosis has been helpful rather than harmful, because as animals they can live more fully than was possible when they were human. One could reasonably contend that the repeated refusal of change—"Je ne veux point changer d'état"—springs from a profound *connaissance de soi* and is grounded in the poem's internal logic: for these creatures it is far better to be a quadruped who enjoys living than to be a pitiful, wind-blown human being for whom life, reduced to the hardships of perpetual travel, is an ordeal to be endured. These animals have learned the lesson La Fontaine imparts in his grandiose farewell fable, "Le Juge arbitre, l'hospitalier, et le solitaire" (XII, 29): "Apprendre à se connaître est le premier des soins / Qu'impose à tous mortels la Majesté suprême."

According to Pierre Clarac, La Fontaine "condamne l'obstination de ces égarés qui, pour suivre leurs passions, renoncent à la dignité humaine et à la gloire."[22] If so, the poet does this in light of values transported from the physical world. Given the empty alternative Ulysses has extended to them, these characters are by no means *égarés*. On the contrary, we readers are misguided if we insist on judging them with an anthropocentric yardstick unsuited for measurement in the enchanted world of words they inhabit.

Although the fabulist certainly seems to be denouncing the animals in "Les Compagnons d'Ulysse," charging that "Ils étaient esclaves d'eux-mêmes," his narrative attitude is nonetheless ambiguous. The four lines following the one just quoted, lines overtly aimed at the Duc de Bourgogne, pose a fascinating problem:[23]

Prince, j'aurais voulu vous choisir un sujet
Où je pusse mêler le plaisant à l'utile:
        C'était sans doute un beau projet
        Si ce choix eût été facile.

Characteristically, the poet proclaims his desire to adhere to the Horatian ideal of blending *utile dulci:* he would both educate and please the reader (cf. "En ces sortes de feinte il faut instruire et plaire, / Et conter pour conter me semble peu d'affaire," VI, 1). La Fontaine seems to feel either that his fable is not instructive or that it is not agreeably written. It appears unlikely, at first glance, that the poet could consider the didactic element to be missing; after all, he does end by advising Fénelon's royal pupil that people resembling Ulysses' comrades are "Gens à qui j'impose pour peine / Votre censure et votre haine." Yet as a teaching vehicle this fable has remarkably little force. What pragmatic value did it hold for the little Duc de Bourgogne? For that matter, how much has it offered—in practical terms—to any other reader through the centuries? To profit literally from La Fontaine's counsel we must await the day when somebody's beverage or wand turns us into beasts, for only then will we be in a position to resist the kind of temptation confronting the characters in "Les Compagnons d'Ulysse." In a more general sense, the poem appears to caution us against letting our appetites control our lives. Yes, but which appetites, and in what conditions? Is the lion's interest in the art of self-defense a blind passion? What is there to reproach in the bear's simple existence? In order to avoid being called a glutton like the wolf, is the reader supposed to become a vegetarian—or to eat lamb just once or twice a month?

One has the impression that La Fontaine's avowed concern with utility, here and elsewhere, is little more than a commonplace. The fabulist's moral statements are interesting, not for their substance as such, but for the way they are expressed (for their interaction with textural elements). What really shines in "Les Compagnons d'Ulysse" is *le plaisant*. This poem lends validity to Henri Peyre's thesis that in La Fontaine's works the "morale" is "très subordonnée à l'élément esthétique. . . ."[24] The anecdote of the lion, bear, and wolf does turn out to be a "beau projet" in which the poet, irrespective of judgments advanced in the framing sections of the fable, allows us to hear the testimony of the texture: his well-chosen blend of rhetorical strategies exuberantly sings the merits of metamorphosis.

Implicit in my discussion of "Les Compagnons d'Ulysse" has been the principle of reciprocity: that is, the reader's comprehension of a given poem can be enhanced by consideration of analogous elements in other poems either in the same book or elsewhere in the *Fables*. The decision to group such an array of verse pieces under a single title cannot be called accidental. In the next chapter, I will explore more fully some ironic devices related to the architecture of the *Fables*. After analyzing two thematically linked but physically separated poems, I will deal with organizational components in an entire unit (Book X).

NOTES

1. Karl Beckson and Arthur Ganz, *A Reader's Guide to Literary Terms: A Dictionary* (New York: Farrar, Straus and Giroux, 1960), p. 203.
2. *The Style of La Fontaine's Fables*, p. 42.
3. Furetière, cited by Couton in *F*, p. 441, n. 6, defines *gorge-chaude* as "la viande chaude qu'on donne aux oiseaux [de fauconnerie] du gibier qu'ils ont pris," and *curée* as "le repas qu'on fait faire aux chiens et aux oiseaux après qu'ils ont pris quelque gibier."
4. In his useful edition of the *Fables* (Paris: Hachette, 1929), René Radouant quotes this passage from Pilpay, *Le Livre des*

lumières ou la conduite des rois: "L'écrevisse, soupçonnant la traîtrise de la grue [note our poet's choice of a different antagonist], se fait porter par elle à l'endroit où elle a mis à l'abri les poissons et profite de l'occasion pour l'étrangler" (p. 389).

5. Cf. "peuple croassant," II, 4; "peuple souriquois," IV, 6 and XII, 8; "peuple rat," VII, 3; "peuple chat," VII, 3; "peuple Vautour," VII, 7; "peuple pigeon," VII, 7; "Peuple caméléon, peuple singe du maître," VIII, 14; "Peuple bêlant," XII, 9.

6. "The Art of Allegory in La Fontaine's Fables," p. 1131.

7. A similar version of my remarks on this poem was published as "La Fontaine's 'Compagnons d'Ulysse': The Merits of Metamorphosis," *French Review,* 53 (1980), 239–47.

8. *Principles of Literary Criticism* (1925; rpt. New York: Harcourt, Brace & World, n.d.), p. 267.

9. René Wellek and Austin Warren, *Theory of Literature,* new rev. ed. (New York: Harcourt, Brace & World, 1956), p. 156; see chapter 12 ("The Mode of Existence of a Literary Work of Art"), pp. 142–57. See also David Daiches, "The Literary Use of Language," chapter 2 of *A Study of Literature for Readers and Critics* (1948; rpt. New York: W. W. Norton, 1964), pp. 21–46; the introduction to the section entitled "The Formalistic Approach: Literature as Aesthetic Structure," in *Five Approaches of Literary Criticism,* ed. Wilbur Scott (New York: Collier Books, 1962), pp. 179–84; Robert Champigny, "Poésie et ontologie," *Poetic Theory/Poetic Practice,* ed. Robert Scholes (Iowa City: MMLA, 1969), pp. 32–35.

10. "Le Douzième Livre des *Fables,*" *Cahiers de l'Association Internationale des Etudes Françaises,* No. 26 (May 1974), p. 108.

11. "Four Modes of Double Irony in La Fontaine's *Fables,*" pp. 208–09.

12. Couton suggests other possible sources of inspiration, pointing out that "l'idée de faire préférer par les victimes de Circé leur condition animale à leur condition humaine apparaît pour la première fois dans Plutarque, *Oeuvres morales, Que les bêtes brutes usent de raison . . . .* Elle est reprise par Gelli, *Circé . . . ,* et par Machiavel, *L'Ane d'or*" (*F,* p. 535, n. 1.

13. *The Style of La Fontaine's Fables,* p. 110.

14. Couton indicates a second possible source of this concept—

Bossuet's *Politique:* "Les hommes, naturellement loups les uns aux autres" (*F,* p. 536, n. 8). In *La Fontaine: Poet and Counterpoet,* Margaret Guiton asserts that in this poem "La Fontaine is covertly attacking the anthropocentric premises of fable symbolism: the manifest absurdity of the human use of the wolf as a symbol of cruelty" (p. 119).

15. To be sure, these two alternatives, contained by the poem, have nothing to do with the social structure of flesh-and-blood humans and wolves. As Wellek and Warren have stated, "A character in a novel [their point is germane for any genre] grows only out of the units of meaning, is made of the sentences either pronounced by the figure or pronounced about it. It has an indeterminate structure in comparison with a biological person who has his coherent past" (*Theory of Literature,* p. 153).

16. Pierre Clarac sees in this "réquisitoire du loup contre la cruauté humaine" a "dissonance remarquable à l'intérieur d'un apologue qui tend à opposer la noblesse de la condition humaine à la bassesse des instincts animaux" ("Variations de La Fontaine dans les six derniers livres des *Fables,"* *L'Information Littéraire* [Jan.–Feb. 1951], pp. 6–7, n. 26). That the poet uncharacteristically leaves the disharmony unresolved must finally be considered, it would seem, a structural weakness in the poem.

17. Couton gives this commentary on *lôs:* "Vieux mot qui est soit noble, soit teinté de burlesque, suivant le contexte. Ici, coloris épique" (*F,* p. 536, n. 10); Radouant cites this definition from the 1694 *Dictionnaire de l'Académie Française:* "Vieux mot, qui signifie louange et qui n'est plus en usage que dans le burlesque" (*Fables,* p. 454, n. 6).

18. *Le Goût de La Fontaine,* p. 247.

19. "Fondement et mode de l'éthique dans les *Fables* de La Fontaine," p. 337. "Nul doute," Périvier contends, "que La Fontaine ne soit lui-même tenté par cette innocence animale," though he does not indicate how one might successfully refute the contradictory framing comments. Périvier elaborates in the following manner the ethical position ostensibly implied in "Les Compagnons d'Ulysse": "Seuls sont à la fois hommes et libres, mais d'une autre liberté, de celle de l'esprit, le héros comme Ulysse, le sage [in *Les Amours de Psyché et de*

Cupidon] et le saint (XII, 29). *Pauci electi*. Les autres ne seront pas sauvés. Ils agissent en loups, et ne peuvent agir autrement. Mais le mal que le loup ne sait pas qu'il fait, eux, ils le *savent*. Telle est, croyons-nous, pour La Fontaine, le fondement spirituel et rationnel de la culpabilité de l'homme" (pp. 337–38). Here the critic is raising moral issues that, though interesting in their own right, go well beyond the implications of the poem being examined.

20. Rubin does, however, make an interesting case for the poem's "double irony": "The real issue . . . is not the relative merit of reason or passion, but the conflict between different hierarchies of value. For Ulysses, the privileged quality is human dignity, which is absolutely inseparable from the form that distinguishes man in appearance from what our hero might call 'the lower orders.' Abandonment of that form entails forfeiture of rank, purely and simply. For the *compagnons,* however, human dignity is either a sham or an irrelevancy, especially when compared with the merits of their current condition" ("Four Modes of Double Irony in La Fontaine's *Fables,*" p. 209; see p. 210 for other comments on the poem's unresolved ironic structure).

21. "Le Douzième Livre des *Fables,*" p. 109.

22. "Variations," p. 6.

23. I am grateful to Stirling Haig for opening this line of inquiry.

24. *Qu'est-ce que le classicisme?,* rev. ed., p. 127; Peyre qualifies "l'élément esthétique" to mean the "désir de 'peindre d'après nature' en restant toujours soucieux du vrai et du beau plus que du bien."

V

Irony and Architecture

The following definition of *architecture,* simple but sufficiently precise, will serve as a convenient point of departure for my remarks in this chapter: "Any design or orderly arrangement perceived by man" (*The American Heritage Dictionary of the English Language*). This basic definition seems acceptable for several reasons: 1) it is broad enough to accommodate any number of approaches to the *Fables;* 2) it frees the critic from the futile task of trying to demonstrate that the patterns discovered conform to the conscious aims of the poet, whatever these objectives may have been; 3) it allows us to emphasize the creative role of the reader or critic; and 4) it reminds us at the same time that fanciful invention will have no part to play in the process, because the posited arrangement or design must be an object of perception.

My fundamental assumption for purposes of the present inquiry is that the *Fables* constitute a system, a highly complex network of interrelationships functioning on many levels. If this is indeed the case, one very meaningful way of reading the *Fables* will involve efforts to identify and interpret the interlocking elements. Our understanding of the *Fables* can be enhanced by a consideration of individual poems in a broader and deeper esthetic perspective. My ancillary assumption is that greater awareness of the architectural principles informing the *Fables* will provide insights into the subtle functioning of La Fontaine's ironic imagination.

In trying to discover whether the *Fables* were composed and organized in accordance with an underlying conceptual design, one receives very little direct assistance from the fabulist himself. No statement of authorial intentions takes precedence over the evidence of the text itself, though the reader is free to consider such remarks for what they may be worth. In the case of La Fontaine, however, we seldom know what his intentions were concerning specific compositional problems, and his reasons for organizing the *Fables* as he did were buried with him. As Georges Couton has written in reference to the arrangement of the poems in the *premier recueil:*

> Le volume est distribué en livres, à l'imitation de Phèdre. Quant aux raisons qui ont amené la répartition des fables entre les six livres et à l'intérieur de chaque livre, nous ne savons rien. Cette disposition vise-t-elle à organiser chaque livre, à lui donner une unité? Le problème a été soulevé, mais non résolu. *(F,* p. xv)

As will be seen, a number of scholars have explored problems relating to the architecture of the *Fables* with varied and often illuminating results, but almost as many significant questions remain to be answered as when Couton wrote the above words more than twenty years ago.

A brief survey of attempts to capture the essence of La Fontaine's architectonic skill should no doubt begin with Leo Spitzer's ground-breaking essay on our poet's "art of transition," first published in 1938 by *PMLA.*[1] Highlighting the Lafontainian "mirror-principle" judged to be "inherent in all fables," with reference to "Le Héron—La Fille" (VII, 4), Spitzer implicitly raises the complex issue of the "fables doubles," to be studied extensively a number of years later, as indicated below, by Jean-Pierre Collinet (see Spitzer, pp. 183–85). Issuing a tacit invitation to fellow scholars, Spitzer asserts: "Many critics have failed to see how tightly controlled every element is in La Fontaine's fables, ruled down to the smallest detail by the technique of transition and organic connection" (p. 185). To respond literally to the challenge contained in this remark would require a work of many volumes, but Spitzer's best insights in his essay on La Fontaine are a welcome harbinger. For him, the "technique of transition" in La Fontaine has more than exegetical implications, being "finally the expression of a world-view that perceives transitions, convergences and correspondences between all things" (p. 200). Contrasting La Fontaine's literary stance with "Boileau's moralising, rhetorical and argumentative manner," Spitzer contends that the fabulist's "fluidity . . . expresses a view of man's action in the world as from a tower of artistic irony . . ." (p. 204), though—as is so often the case when critics write of purportedly ironic events and situations—he fails to specify the meaning he wishes to attribute to the term; therefore the reader does not have a clear idea of how, in Spitzer's estimation, the "technique of transition" he recognizes in the *Fables* might be related to La Fontaine's overall ironic outlook.

By implication, Spitzer imparts a salutary warning to those who will examine the architecture of the *Fables:* while paying close attention to an encompassing verbal design that may link poems with each other, critics must not lose sight of the governing dynamics responsible for making every fable an integrated act of creativity. In addition to obeying certain "general laws" (not only "the technique of transition" but also "the antinomy between the laconic and the digressive" and "the law of variation"), "each fable," according to Spitzer, remains "a self-enclosed whole with an individual construction, its own specific proportions and its own set of internal correspondences . . ." (pp. 205–06). It is essential never to allow the momentum generated by a theory of compositional system to mask the differentiating qualities that make each poem unique and worthy of explication in its own right.

In a monograph on La Fontaine's early artistic growth, published in 1952, Philip A. Wadsworth called attention to the architecture of the *Fables* of 1668. He suggested that the poet's "musicianship" is the key to this problem in the first six books, which Wadsworth calls ". . . a complex symphony in six nonchalant but harmonically perfect movements."[2] Close examination of this interesting possibility seems to await the arrival of a student of French literature with a solid background in musicology. In the same study, Wadsworth underscores the importance of poems occupying the initial and final positions in Books I–VI, while noting that "the internal organization of each book is far more elusive" (p. 215).

A wide variety of subjects meriting treatment by scholars are cited by Pierre Moreau in his 1960 study of the first collection of *Fables;* some of these topics involve what may be termed architectural aspects.[3] One such topic, later to be elaborated by Jean-Pierre Collinet under the rubric "fables doubles," concerns what Moreau terms the "diptyques de fables" (for instance, "La Mort et le malheureux" and "La Mort et le bûcheron," I, 15 and 16; or "Le Pâtre et le lion" and "Le Lion et le chasseur," VI, 1 and 2).

A very different strategy for attempting to discover the "design or orderly arrangement" of the *Fables* is that adopted by René Jasinski, from whose politically oriented viewpoint the fables of Books I–VI reflect the activities and attitudes of two of La Fontaine's noted contemporaries: the poet's former patron, the disgraced Nicolas Fouquet; and the triumphant finance minister, Jean-Baptiste Colbert.[4] Pierre Bornecque has likewise found tempting the construction of imagined parallels between the universe of the *Fables* and real-life society in the age of the Sun-King,[5] but such endeavors do not advance our understanding of the esthetic architecture of the *Fables* because approaches based on contemporary allusions (many of them hopelessly cryptic, moreover) lead us finally away from the texts rather than into them.

A more illuminating approach, mentioned above (chapter III, note 31), is that developed by Jacques-Henri Périvier in an article concerned with "La Cigale et la fourmi" as a thematic introduction to the *Fables*. Périvier argues that in this initial fable we find in juxtaposition La Fontaine's two fundamental visions, "la vision réaliste et comique" and "la vision poétique et lyrique," which are operative, he believes, in the *Contes* and *Oeuvres diverses* as well as in the *Fables*. It would no doubt be necessary to define these terms more sharply, and perhaps to modify them somewhat, in order to apply them in an investigation of linking elements throughout the twelve books, but these two "visions" do suggest a potentially useful technique for determining interrelationships between and among fables.

Ideally, a thorough consideration of internal architectural patterns in the *Fables* would come to terms with the harmonizing orchestration of all the poems throughout the twelve books—if indeed so many seemingly diverse elements can plausibly be perceived as structurally harmonious. Until the perhaps distant day when such a monumental challenge is satisfactorily addressed, less ambitious efforts can cast a good deal of light on integrative aspects of La Fontaine's art. As already suggested, Jean-Pierre Collinet has greatly enhanced our understanding of the structural richness of the *Fables* through his careful study of the poet's "fables doubles."[6] When he introduces the problem of constructing a Lafontainian *thématique*, Collinet, in words reminiscent of Spitzer's foresight, writes of La Fontaine's "art de la variation" by which the author weaves, within and among his works, "un réseau de correspondances qui manifestent une continuité secrète sous l'apparente dispersion, et soulignent l'unité profonde de la création poétique" (p. 14). In his conclusion, Collinet properly points out that much remains to be accomplished toward the full development of a *thématique* of La Fontaine's works. In his view, "L'important serait moins de répertorier les thèmes—aussi bien l'entreprise serait infinie—que d'étudier comment ils se groupent et se développent" (pp. 423–24). That the problem deserves more than a schematic treatment is illustrated by Pierre Bornecque's examination of what he calls the "double entrelacement" of the *Fables:* the development of sixty-two themes in more than two hundred poems, and the supposed thematic organization of the twelve books.[7] Bornecque himself recognizes the limitations of his rapid survey of "le monde des thèmes": "Il faudrait . . . une très longue étude, que l'étroitesse de ce cadre m'interdit, pour résoudre complètement le problème de l'entrelacement des thèmes et de l'organisation des livres" (p. 102).

Recently, in a more convincing presentation, Georges Couton has built a judicious case for Epicureanism as the controlling element in one book of the *Fables.*[8] Even if this fine exercise in traditional thematic scholarship does not become a seminal essay in an age of new critical directions, it may for now at least be reasonable, when undertaking studies of Lafontainian architecture, to heed Couton's cautionary remark that ". . . la lecture la plus profitable des *Fables,* en l'état actuel des études sur La Fontaine, est celle qui s'astreint à les prendre livre par livre" (p. 290). I hope that my reading of Book X in this chapter will help substantiate the usefulness of this advice; on the other hand, by comparing "La Chatte métamorphosée en femme" (II, 18) with "La Souris métamorphosée en fille" (IX, 7) I will try to show that investigation of the "fables doubles" remains a potentially fruitful approach to one facet of poetic organization. First, however, I would like to pass in review the work of scholars who, like Georges Couton, have sought to uncover signs of La Fontaine's patterning dexterity at the level of individual books.

Earlier, in *La Politique de La Fontaine,* Couton himself had studied the thematic disposition of Book X (his model will be cited again later in this chapter); he recapitulates his tripartite organization of these themes in his "Introduction" to the Classiques Garnier edition of the *Fables:* "dans le livre X, mise en accusation de l'homme par les bêtes, thème de l'aventure, thème de la condition royale" (*F*, p. xxvii). The convention of publishing these fables in books has been treated by Jacques Proust in an essay developed in a broader context.[9] According to Proust, the arrangement by books of these poems is by no means haphazard in that "son désordre apparent recèle et dévoile tout à la fois un ordre profond"; he finds the order thus revealed to be

> à l'image de l'univers de La Fontaine, régi par la loi fondamentale de l'opposition des contraires et celle de l'analogie qui en dérive. Autrement dit, cette disposition n'est ni aléatoire, ni décorative, mais aussi significative que les autres parties de l'oeuvre. (p. 232)

Comprehending these "laws" of literary composition, with their subtle counterpoint of contraries and likenesses, will involve learning to read *"entre les fables, comme nous avons appris à lire les fables"* (p. 232). Near the end of his article, Proust argues that an "étude d'ensemble" written along these lines should ultimately be expanded beyond the framework of individual books of poems: "Il serait curieux de voir comment deux fables parentes s'éclairent mutuellement à distance, comment aussi leur signification intrinsèque est modifiée, selon le cycle auquel la disposition par livres les rattache" (p. 248). Others, however, have decided to focus on the design of individual books.

Philip A. Wadsworth's incisive essay on Book XII, quoted in chapter IV, raises a number of issues from the perspective of literary history. Solving certain problems associated with the organization of Book XII may prove particularly challenging to anyone who follows Wadsworth's lead, because he indicates that the questions he poses in the article are designed to show "combien nous sommes loin de comprendre la pensée intime de La Fontaine" (p. 103). Furthermore, he declares: "L'architecture du douzième livre est assez déroutante, puisqu'il est agrandi par des pièces diverses dont la composition s'échelonne sur une période d'au moins quinze ans" (p. 105). Perhaps a researcher bold enough to accept the task of looking for structural harmonies in Book XII amid apparent fortuitousness ought to begin with a radical application of the theories of Jacques Proust cited above.

Two essays in a recent issue of *L'Esprit Créateur* devoted to the works of La Fontaine (and edited by David Lee Rubin) deal with internal arrangements in separate books of the *Fables*. Nathan Gross analyzes the epic elements pervading Book VI, whereas, drawing on a notion introduced by Alain-Marie Bassy, I probe the figurative as well as the literal dimensions of the figure of the labyrinth in Book X.[10] That such divergent approaches can coexist peacefully in the many-storied fable-house that La Fontaine constructed would seem in itself to be a clear indication of the poet's extraordinary workmanship.

The rest of this chapter is primarily an attempt to establish, through a close reading of selected poems, that certain architectural patterns in the *Fables* are symbiotically connected to La Fontaine's ironic vision.

For the purposes of explication, all the writings of La Fontaine, irrespective of their origins in time (dates of composition, if known, and of initial publication), share the same temporal plane. As Pierre Malandain states in his fascinating book on intertextuality in the *Fables*, invoking Roland Barthes's work on Michelet: "[O]n considérera tous les éléments de l'oeuvre comme contemporains." In his view, the appropriate strategy is to read "l'oeuvre comme signifiant plus par la spécificité de ses paradigmes que par l'organisation linéaire de son existence syntagmatique, diachronique."[11] Thus it is perfectly legitimate to confront a pair of poems historically separated by the one-decade gap between the first and second *recueils*.

The two fables in question here, positioned by the poet in Books II and IX, are mentioned as a couple—but not analyzed—by Jean-Pierre Collinet in his chapter on the "fables doubles" in *Le Monde littéraire de La Fontaine* (p. 226). The very titles of these poems unmistakably invite the reader to compare the texts: "La Chatte métamorphosée en femme" and "La Souris métamorphosée en fille" are tantalizingly parallel headings. From the outset we know that both situations are to involve the transformation of animals into (female) human beings. Recalling La Fontaine's fondness for humorous reversals, one has logical grounds for assuming that these metamorphoses will not be permanent. One can cite in tentative support of this hypothesis the case of the hapless fox in "Le Loup et le renard" (XII, 9), who tries in vain to acquire the efficacious food-gathering habits of wolves by wrapping himself in the skin of a dead wolf. The narrator's comment on the fox's failure would appear to be broadly applicable to analogous episodes:

> Que sert-il qu'on se contrefasse?
> Prétendre ainsi changer est une illusion:
> L'on reprend sa première trace
> A la première occasion.

Our temptation to treat these lines as a stable generalization is undermined, however, by the example of Ulysses' companions who, in the first poem of this final book, have been able (as will be recalled) to preserve unmodified their common resolve to continue living as beasts ("Je ne veux point changer d'état"). Indeed, there is often more (or perhaps less) to La Fontaine's cleanly crafted moral statements than meets the eye. Therefore, though the reader's prediction concerning the cat-woman and mouse-girl poems will be proved accurate, we begin reading them with our title-based expectations a little insecure.

Someone with interests different from mine could use these two fables to illustrate the influences exercised by the addition of new sources for the poems of 1678–79.

The fabulist La Fontaine is never in artistic bondage to his predecessors, of course, but it is true that "La Chatte métamorphosée en femme," based on Aesop, contains only forty-two lines and has a relatively simple structure, whereas "La Souris métamorphosée en fille," based on Bidpai (Pilpay), is eighty lines long, anecdotally more complex, and comprises an elaborate philosophical development. Surface differences aside, a paired reading of these poems reveals a whole network of intriguing similarities and contrasts.

Both in "La Chatte" and in "La Souris" (to abbreviate their titles for convenience), the narrator provides opportunities for the reader to contemplate the unfolding action from an ironic vantage point. From the first lines of "La Chatte," a man wildly in love with his cat is set up as the probable victim of the law of inevitable reversion to type, though he is confidently unaware of his future predicament:

> Un Homme chérissait éperdument sa Chatte;
> Il la trouvait mignonne, et belle, et délicate,
>   Qui miaulait d'un ton fort doux.
>   Il était plus fou que les fous.

Line one, while alliteratively embracing verb and object, seems to trigger significant etymological echoes; this man loved his pet very dearly but did not realize how nature would conspire against his affection, *cher* evoking *aimé* and *précieux* but also *coûteux* (he would pay for his infatuation); the adverb *éperdument* appropriately mirrors its origin in an Old French verb meaning *perdre complètement* (*NDE*, pp. 160 and 269). The adjective *mignonne* is also aptly chosen: besides emphasizing a typical motive for human passion, it hints at the species of the man's love-object through word association, being related to *minet* by way of their common source in the popular Gallo-Roman word *mine* 'cat' (*NDE*, pp. 464 and 466). However *mig-*

nonne she may be in the eyes of her master, *minette* she was born and will in blood and bones continue to be. And her sweet meowing reminds us that her beauty and delicateness are feline charms, not necessarily better or worse than human traits but fundamentally different.

Without delay the man is pictured revealing by his actions why he has been called madder than those literally insane. Resorting to prayers, tears, and magical formulas, the love-ridden fellow

> Fait tant qu'il obtient du destin
> Que sa Chatte en un beau matin
> Devient femme, et le matin même,
> Maître sot en fait sa moitié.
> Le voilà fou d'amour extrême,
> De fou qu'il était d'amitié.

The phrase *maître sot* rings with ironic resonances. Master of no one (the bride, née *chatte*, only appears to be his—"*sa* moitié"), the man deserves the title *maître* only if he is to be designated an incomparable fool. At the same time, *sot*, as every *dix-septiémiste* knows, can carry more than one meaning or connotation in a neoclassical text: it can signify *vivement épris* or *fou*, to be sure, but also *dupe* and *mari trompé* (see Dubois and Lagane, p. 453). Our bridegroom's invincible rival, foreshadowed here, will not be a tomcat but rather inbred animal behavior.

The character in "La Souris" whose role to an extent parallels that of the man in "La Chatte" is a *Bramin* (a Hindu priest according to Furetière, quoted by Couton: *F*, p. 502, n. 2). The narrator treats the Brahmin with considerably more respect than that accorded the *fou* of the other poem:

> Une Souris tomba du bec d'un Chat-Huant:
>   Je ne l'eusse pas ramassée;
> Mais un Bramin le fit; je le crois aisément:
>   Chaque pays a sa pensée.

Whereas the fabulist (as persona) can redeem the Brahmin's curious act by having recourse to relativism, he could find no such means of salvaging the cat-woman's "hypocondre de mari" (her "bizarre husband," as he calls the man at one point). The narrator proceeds to explain the philosophical basis of the Brahmins' fondness for such creatures as mice—their belief in metempsychosis (the transmigration of souls):

> ils ont en tête
> Que notre âme au sortir d'un Roi,
> Entre dans un ciron, ou dans telle autre bête
> Qu'il plaît au Sort. C'est là l'un des points de leur loi.

Under these circumstances, it does not seem strange to find the Brahmin begging a sorcerer to lodge the mouse (that is, her soul) "Dans un corps qu'elle eût eu pour hôte au temps jadis." Presumably operating on the assumption that the mouse had once been alive in human form, the wizard, an amusingly perfect choice as the agent of this metamorphosis (compare, phonetically, *sorcier* and *souris*), changes the little rodent into a fifteen-year-old girl whom the Trojan prince Paris would have considered to be more appealing than Helen (". . . le fils de Priam pour elle aurait tenté / Plus encor qu'il ne fit pour la grecque beauté").

Unlike the laughable male protagonist of "La Chatte," however, the Brahmin thinks of marriage only in order to enable the young lady to select her own spouse: "Il dit à cet objet si doux: / Vous n'avez qu'à choisir; car chacun est jaloux / De l'honneur d'être votre époux." Without a pause she announces her willingness to give "Ma voix au plus puissant de tous." The man in the other fable had been overtly cast as the ironist's most obvious victim from the start, but it is only now that the Brahmin begins to be tacitly judged from the narrator's perch of greater knowledge. Thinking of power in purely physical terms, the Brahmin exclaims that the sun will be his son-in-law ("notre gen-dre"). But the sun realizes that the dense cloud, capable of hiding him from view, is more powerful still. The wedding bells will not yet chime, however, because the cloud knows that the wind can blow him about at will. Making no effort to conceal his impatience, the Brahmin summons this pro-spective conqueror of the mouse-girl's heart: 'O vent donc, puisque vent y a, / Viens dans les bras de notre belle." When the wind hastens forth, however, he is halted by a mountain. Even this towering mass of earth does not prove to be the most powerful suitor; if he agreed to marry the girl, he says, he would face a quarrel with the rat, and the latter is able to pierce his surface (thanks, although it is not stated, to his teeth and claws).

Here the fable joins its counterpart in Book II: "Au mot de Rat, la Damoiselle / Ouvrit l'oreille; il fut l'époux." Similarly, the honeymoon of the cat-woman in the other poem had been disturbed by the presence of a few mice—a very tempting presence, from the bride's innately feline point of view: "Aussitôt la femme est sur pieds: / Elle manqua son aventure. / Souris de revenir, femme d'être en posture." Nature causes the once-and-future mouse to react to the spoken reference to a rat in the same way that nature prompts the once-and-future cat to spring in pur-suit when confronted with the sight of mice. The unfortu-nate husband having been left in oblivion from the time of the cat-and-mouse game in "La Chatte," the fabulist con-cludes the poem with a kind of aphoristic overkill by way of a fourteen-line passage expressing from various angles the irrepressible force of nature. On the other hand, the resolution of "La Souris" is much less clear-cut. While acknowledging in an analogous manner the predictably strong attraction of kindred spirits for one another ("On tient toujours du lieu dont on vient"), the narrator is aware that the anecdote of the mouse-girl and the rat contains a little "sophisme" and thus may ultimately prove little if anything about relative strengths and weaknesses in general terms: "Car quel époux n'est point au Soleil préférable / En s'y prenant ainsi? Dirai-je qu'un géant / Est moins fort qu'une puce? elle le mord pourtant." In other words, it would seem that with this line of reasoning the poet is hinting at the inherently tenuous nature of many of our judgments; on a covert level, he may even be aiming at his own lesson-giving self (and at readers naive enough to take deceptively pithy verses at face value) a bit of criticism for giving the impression that the final meaning of interpersonal relationships, as portrayed in stylized fashion from fable to fable, can be neatly captured in poetic maxims. He notes, furthermore, that in the present instance it was an arbitrary decision to stop the story of power and weakness with the rat at the summit of strength over others:

> Le Rat devait aussi renvoyer, pour bien faire,
>   La belle au chat, le chat au chien,
>   Le chien au loup. Par le moyen
>   De cet argument circulaire,
> Pilpay jusqu'au Soleil eût enfin remonté;
> Le Soleil eût joui de la jeune beauté.

To employ the terms of the Ethiopian metaphor (see *A Rhetoric of Irony*, p. 40), when the wax of illusion has melted away (in this case the false inference of the rat's absolute supremacy over sun, cloud, wind, and mountain), what remains is the gold of a broadly applicable ironic message: that one is unwise to seek universal truths in fables whose import, in aphoristic terms, may be no less fragmentary than the anecdote the poet has chosen to present, selecting certain details (chiefly for artistic, rather than moralistic, effects) while suppressing others. Therefore, the tale of the mouse-girl and the rat, which, according to the narrator, "Prouve assez bien ce point" that "On tient toujours du lieu dont on vient," does not establish its validity for general purposes any more successfully than the poem of the cat-woman proves for all time and circumstances the unassailable grip of natural instinct (one can imagine, for instance, a scenario in which the woman, relieved to be able to enjoy "le plaisir des nouveaux mariés" with her husband, and to be rid of her mice-chasing mania, happily joins the lion, bear and wolf of poem XII, 1 in refusing to "changer d'état").

At the end of "La Souris" (lines 60–80), La Fontaine refers to the case of the failed metamorphosis of the mouse into a psychologically adapted human being as a means of attacking the doctrine of metempsychosis. He argues that the sorcerer's deed, "loin de la prouver, fait voir sa fausseté." He relies on close observation of behavior to demonstrate the inadequacy of the Brahmin's philosophical system, according to which it is necessary

> Que l'homme, la souris, le ver, enfin chacun
> Aille puiser son âme en un trésor commun:
>> Toutes sont donc de même trempe;
>> Mais agissant diversement
>> Selon l'organe seulement
>> L'une s'élève, et l'autre rampe.

One must be very cautious, however, in deciding whether to take such statements at face value. It is entirely possible that the man Jean de La Fontaine considered the idea of reincarnation to be utter nonsense, but that is beside the point in the context of the above lines. From what we know of his literary persona, the narrative self in La Fontaine is not a confused mind, yet a literal reading of his denunciation of the Brahmin leads directly to the conclusion that for him literature and life are ontologically identical. But we can be certain that the *maître des eaux et forêts* of Château-Thierry who, as author, wrote "Tout parle en mon Ouvrage, et même les Poissons" ("A Monseigneur le Dauphin," *F*, p. 31), was well aware of the differences. The zoological fact that worms crawl whereas people stand erect has no bearing on patterns of conduct in the *Fables,* where all characters are at the mercy of the poet's imagination. The fabulist could not have thought anyone would take seriously a refutation of the doctrine of the transmigration of souls based on a story in which a mouse becomes a girl of fifteen, a mountain is afraid of offending a rat, a cloud speaks of his inability to escape the wind's breath, and the sun is viewed as a possible son-in-law. Thus there is no empirical value in the narrator's answer to his own question concerning why the mouse in a girl's body became the rat's prize:

> D'où vient donc que ce corps si bien organisé
> > Ne put obliger son hôtesse
> De s'unir au Soleil, un Rat eut sa tendresse?
> > Tout débattu, tout bien pesé,
> Les âmes des souris et les âmes des belles
> > Sont très différentes entre elles.

The organisms introduced in this fable (or in any other) are not related to those in the physical world except by analogy. The link between them has a linguistic foundation. When, in reference to the bruised mouse falling from an owl's beak, the narrator exclaims, "Je ne l'eusse pas ramassée," he is making humorous capital of the literary convention allowing him to create the illusion that this rodent belongs to genus *Mus;* he appears to be saying, in effect, "Although you and I are aware, dear reader, that taxonomic nomenclature is out of place in a poem, let's pretend—just for fun—that this mouse is really wounded and not just a six-letter, two-syllable word." Beyond (and above) his ostensible debate about reincarnation with a Hindu priest, the narrator achieves balance and vocal harmony in his pairing of *âmes des souris* with *âmes des belles,* and the four closing lines, while begging several epistemological questions, fittingly summarize nothing more than the mouse-girl's fancifully expounded recidivism:

Il en faut revenir toujours à son destin.
C'est-à-dire, à la loi par le Ciel établie.
   Parlez au diable, employez la magie,
Vous ne détournerez nul être de sa fin.

A retrospective reading of the other metamorphosis poem being examined in light of this one seems to confirm that the overt message about the power of *le naturel* stemming from the cat-woman's experience masks a complex dialectic: of *le naturel* we read (in "La Chatte"), "Il se moque de tout, certain âge accompli," but the qualifier in the second hemistich is critical, suggesting, contrary to the thematic thrust of the anecdote (in which the man is characterized as *fou, sot,* and *hypocondre* because he consents to marry a woman who used to be a cat, not a cat old enough to remember her past or a cat *sui generis* but purely and simply a *cat),* that in the right conditions this kind of transformation just might be successful. Is the stable didacticism seemingly present in the text not thereby being sabotaged via the language of the text itself? And is it by accident that this fable's counterpart in Book IX is immediately followed by a strikingly ironic poem titled "Le Fou qui vend la sagesse" (IX, 8)? When La Fontaine states, in its opening verses, "Jamais auprès des fous ne te mets à portée. / Je ne te puis donner un plus sage conseil," is he not looking back with a wry gaze at the preceding fable as well as ahead in order to set the stage for the lines to follow? And who might be the fool selling wisdom in "La Souris"? The Brahmin, whose alleged wisdom concerning metempsychosis our narrator considers bogus? Pythagoras, the Greek philosopher who is said to have been responsible for making this Indian doctrine known in his own country and, indirectly, throughout the West ("Pythagore chez eux a puisé ce mystère")? Or could this even be an instance of playful self-parody in which the fabulist covertly undercuts the conclusion so confidently drawn from the events of the mouse-girl episode, thereby hinting through the technique of cross-reference that "Les Fables ne sont pas ce qu'elles semblent être" (VI, 1)? Forty-five years after Leo Spitzer's landmark essay, we still have much to learn about Lafontainian transitions.

It will be instructive to approach the problem of textual modulation in the *Fables* from another angle. Moving from implicitly paired poems to an entire unit, I will now examine the irony and architecture of Book X, whose fifteen poems hold many clues to La Fontaine's remarkable skill as a builder of verbal edifices.

First of all, the fables in Book X are well suited to the testing of a potentially fertile hypothesis: that the pivotal figure unifying the disparate elements of the *Fables* is the labyrinth, an idea adumbrated a few years ago by Alain-Marie Bassy,[12] who contends:

> Chaque fable en effet ne marque qu'une étape dans l'itinéraire total. Elle annule et périme une "moralité" tirée auparavant, elle sera à son tour surpassée par une autre. Quel que soit l'itinéraire choisi, la découverte de la leçon finale [given in "Le Juge arbitre, l'hospitalier, et le solitaire," XII, 29] exige qu'on ne s'arrête point à l'une des stations, mais qu'on poursuive la quête jusqu'au bout. . . . (p. 19)

Only at the end of Book XII, in Bassy's judgment, dòes La Fontaine reveal the sole exit from his literary maze:

> Des trois voies ouvertes encore au bout du parcours, pour qui ne s'est point laissé prendre aux mirages des lointains, une seule mène véritablement à la sortie du labyrinthe: la justice et la charité, au moment ultime, sont encore une fois "surpassées" par la connaissance de soi-même et de ses limites, seule clef du savoir-vivre et du savoir-mourir. Les chemins suivis par le Juge arbitre et par l'Hospitalier recoupent, juste avant la sortie, la voie royale du solitaire, préparée dès longtemps. (p. 20)

Without insisting on the capital importance of this final poem,[13] one may profitably view the labyrinth (in its literal and figurative applications) as one key to the interconnection of the *Fables*.

On the most obvious level the labyrinth is a maze, an entangled construction filled with dead-end passageways. Its minimal characteristic is a virtual absence of escape routes. This figure need not imply either psychological or physical danger (as any fan of a carnival's house of mirrors is aware), but in Book X it often translates as a treacherous enclosure. For instance, in fable 1 ("L'Homme et la couleuvre") it is the sack in which the unreasoning man places his victim, the snake. In fable 3 ("Les Poissons et le cormoran"), which was discussed at some length in chapter IV, this enclosure is the "retraite" where the captive fish stay until, one by one, they are devoured by the cormorant; this bird alludes to the labyrinthine character of the trap when he states, "Nul que Dieu seul et moi n'en connaît les chemins: / Il n'est demeure plus secrète." (This fish-preserve is, incidentally, a labyrinth only for the fish; it has other features ideally suited to the cormorant's needs, being "Transparent, peu creux, fort étroit.") Another form of treacherous den is evoked in fable 6 ("L'Araignée et l'hirondelle"): the spider's web; her woven trap, built from sturdy materials, is potentially as lethal as the cormorant's shallow reservoir, but she does not enjoy his uninterrupted success because of the pesky swallow ("Caracolant, frisant l'air et les eaux, / Elle me prend mes mouches à ma porte"). The notion of confinement likewise appears in fable 7 ("La Perdrix et les coqs"), in which the partridge stoically laments that the 'maître de ces lieux . . . / . . . nous prend avec des tonnelles, / Nous loge avec des Coqs, et nous coupe les ailes." In fable 9 ("Le Berger et le roi"), it is the court, a popular Lafontainian target, that assumes labyrinthine properties. It is a place where, in effect, people of integrity seem on the verge of being blocked in blind alleys of intrigue: "On cabale, on suscite / Accusateurs, et gens grevés par ses arrêts" (those of the shepherd turned "Juge Souverain").

A more subtle and more revealing application of the labyrinth concept in Book X, and throughout the *Fables*, lies in the psychological sphere: numerous characters behave as though their minds were labyrinths, hopelessly impenetrable webworks from which no clear thought can ever emerge. A brief examination of the opening fable, "L'Homme et la couleuvre," will illustrate how the poet deftly develops the mind-as-labyrinth equation.

The man of the title, having spied a certain snake, quickly resolves to kill the beast. The animal's guilt or innocence is not at issue here. Although three witnesses testify in support of the snake's contention that "le symbole des ingrats / Ce n'est point le serpent, c'est l'homme" (it is not coincidental, I think, that the type of reptile playing a role here, the *couleuvre*, is in the biological world nonvenomous), the death sentence is finally carried out.

The poet obliquely hints at the quality of the man's mind in the fourth line when he mentions "l'animal pervers," hastening to clarify: "C'est le serpent que je veux dire, / Et non l'homme: on pourrait aisément s'y tromper." As the story develops, however, the derogatory epithet, *pervers*, projected on a path of ironic indirection, wil in no way fit the snake. The adjective derives from a Latin verb signifying *renverser* or *retourner* (*NDE*, p. 556). The man's mental processes are plainly inverted; his thinking evokes the tangled circuits of a labyrinth.

Hearing the snake's accusation that humans are the most ungrateful creatures of all, the man reacts as though he were trapped in a maze: ". . . Ces paroles / Firent arrê ter l'autre; il recula d'un pas." Although this reverse mo tion betrays the man's evident inability to counter the snake's reasoning, he offers this bald, imperious response "Tes raisons sont frivoles." Haughtily invoking his powe to end the debate at once ("Je pourrais décider, car ce droi m'appartient"), he surprisingly proposes that outside testimony be admitted, to which the snake agrees.

The first informant is a cow, who declares, "La Couleuvre a raison; pourquoi dissimuler?" What has been her reward for nourishing the man and restoring his health?

> Enfin me voilà vieille; il me laisse en un coin
> Sans herbe; s'il voulait encor me laisser paître!
> Mais je suis attachée; et si j'eusse eu pour maître
> Un serpent, eût-il su jamais pousser si loin
> L'ingratitude? Adieu: j'ai dit ce que je pense.

The fabulist skillfully uses run-on lines to stress the man's cruelty to the starving animal *(Sans herbe, L'ingratitude)* and also to underscore the cow's wry preference for what had been labeled an *animal pervers* (the noun *serpent*, visually separated from *maître*, is joined to it aurally and syntactically).

How effectively does the man parry the cow's arguments? With no more aplomb than that exhibited by Ulysses in the first fable of Book XII.

> L'homme, tout étonné d'une telle sentence,
> Dit au Serpent: Faut-il croire ce qu'elle dit?
> C'est une radoteuse; elle a perdu l'esprit.

He is *étonné:* the cow's testimony has left him thunderstruck (cf. Latin *extonare,* from *tonus: tonnerre—NDE,* p. 282). Yet he does not flex under the weight of specific evidence. On the contrary, he casually dismisses the cow as a *radoteuse,* even though her speech displayed no symptoms of senility. Nor does he attempt to indicate what had prompted him to make such a judgment. Instead, he seems willing to defer to the next witness: "Croyons ce Boeuf." And the snake agrees: "Croyons, dit la rampante bête." This descriptive phrase emphasizes a basic difference, in standard zoological terms, between reptiles and people: the former crawl, whereas the latter stand erect and stride; in the present context, however, the horizontal/vertical opposition (often suggestive of inferiority and superiority, respectively) is inverted on the intellectual scale.

As for the ox, how has he benefitted from all the labor expended to help man? Humans have repaid him with "Force coups, peu de gré." And what is typically the experience of oxen who have become elderly? "On croyait l'honorer [that is, a single ox representing the whole species] chaque fois que les hommes / Achetaient de son sang l'indulgence des Dieux." Once again, the man refuses to deal directly with charges brought against him. Instead, he calls for silence:

> Faisons taire
> Cet ennuyeux déclamateur;
> Il cherche de grands mots, et vient ici se faire,
> Au lieu d'arbitre, accusateur.
> Je le récuse aussi. . . .

Here we find another form of reversal: if anyone is ranting, it must be the man. It is obvious now that he had no intention of believing what the ox told him—unless of course the testimony had flattered him or denounced the snake.

The last personage to testify is a tree; its role is suggested by phonetic pairing, for *arbitre* (see above) and *arbre* appear in successive lines. It did the tree no good to protect humankind against heat, rain, and wind; to provide esthetic pleasure as well as shade; to offer loads of fruit, flowers, fireplace logs—"Un rustre l'abattait. . . ."

That all this testimony has been advanced in a futile cause becomes quickly apparent:

> L'Homme trouvant mauvais que l'on l'eût convaincu,
> Voulut à toute force avoir cause gagnée.

Je suis bien bon, dit-il, d'écouter ces gens-là.
Du sac et du serpent aussitôt il donna
   Contre les murs, tant qu'il tua la bête.

The man had willingly entered the labyrinth of juridical rhetoric, but all three paths (those of cow, ox, and tree) had led him to an undesired destination. The goal sought by all participants is justice; however, since the man insists on rejecting any evidence about himself that is not exculpating, he has decided to trace a new passageway across the maze. Equity is whatever he wills it to be; as the snake had said to him early in the poem, ". . . ta justice, / C'est ton utilité, ton plaisir, ton caprice." Reason has conspired against him in vain. For this man, who "Voulut *à toute force* [italics added] avoir cause gagnée," superior strength has replaced a rational response in determining what is right.

But power from one perspective may from another be frailty; as we learned in "La Souris métamorphosée en fille," determining who is the "plus puissant de tous" depends on how one chooses to define the term. The overbearing human in this fable (X, 1) plays with impunity the role of executioner. But he does not win the battle of language. In one of his most famous early fables, "Le Loup et l'agneau" (I, 10), La Fontaine had subtly demonstrated that the initial line, "La raison du plus fort est toujours la meilleure," contradicts the logical thrust of the anecdote itself (unless *best* is interpreted in terms of efficacy). There is a similar, though more discursive, impact at the end of "L'Homme et la couleuvre." After telling how the man killed the snake, the poet adds:

   On en use ainsi chez les grands.
La raison les offense; ils se mettent en tête
Que tout est né pour eux, quadrupèdes, et gens,
   Et serpents.

Si quelqu'un desserre les dents,
C'est un sot.—J'en conviens. Mais que faut-il donc faire?
—Parler de loin, ou bien se taire.

The message itself is banal: it is dangerous to impede the mighty. What is interesting here, as is usually the case in the *Fables,* is the manner in which the poet conveys this notion. The rhyme of *tête* with *bête* calls attention to an inherent similarity between prideful humans and beasts; this recalls the playful reference to an "animal pervers" at the beginning of the poem. The assimilation of humans with nonhumans is further punctuated by the juxtaposition of *quadrupèdes, gens,* and *serpents,* the latter two terms being comically paired in compressed rhyme as an unexpected trisyllabic line follows an alexandrine. By means of the neuter pronoun *tout,* the author succeeds in depersonifying the noun *gens* (compare "tout est né" with "tous sont nés"; it must be admitted, of course, that the second expression may simply have sounded less appropriate to La Fontaine's poetically attuned ears). The placement of the monosyllabic *gens* in the middle of the three-part series, flanked by longer nouns, may also serve to devalue the status of a term representing humanity.

What might the speaker mean when he advises, "Parler de loin, ou bien se taire"?[14] The second half of this octosyllabic lesson seems clear enough: nothing is safer than silence. On the other hand, "Parler de loin" is open to an array of interpretations. On a figurative level, "Parler de loin" suggests verbal remoteness or speaking with irony. Such a survival technique enables the stag of "Les Obsèques de la lionne" (VIII,14) to save his hide, whereupon the fabulist as narrator recommends:

Amusez les Rois par des songes,
Flattez-les, payez-les d'agréables mensonges,
Quelque indignation dont leur coeur soit rempli,
Ils goberont l'appât, vous serez leur ami.

There is no guarantee in the labyrinthine world of the *Fables*, however, that similar strategies would be adequate to save every character from the whims of the powerful. The snake in "L'Homme et la couleuvre" is doomed from the start. The poet has not implied that any amount of logic or ironic language or passive resistance would have stayed the brutal execution. That being the case, "Parler de loin" assumes an esthetic meaning: the author, as literary persona, can strike at his targets with linguistic indirectness. From this perspective, the phrase "Si quelqu'un desserre les dents, / C'est un sot" is richly evocative. Ostensibly, La Fontaine is telling us that anyone encountering strong adversaries would be foolish to argue with them. But he is also accurately describing the behavior of the man in this fable, a character whose speech betrays his inability to render an objective assessment of what he has heard (the cow is not a *radoteuse*, nor does the ox deserve to be called an "ennuyeux déclamateur"); when this man speaks, his mindless utterances amount to no more than the unclenching of teeth—mechanical gestures devoid of human qualities. It is this man, rather than his animal and vegetal opponents, who becomes a ludicrous figure ("C'est un sot") whenever he opens his mouth. He may win the battle of physical force, but he loses decisively the war of words and wit.

The second fable of Book X likewise elaborates the mind-as-labyrinth metaphor. The central action of this poem, "La Tortue et les deux canards," amusingly demonstrates the proposition discussed above: "Si quelqu'un desserre les dents, / C'est un sot" (or, in this instance, *une sotte*).[15] Though the hollow maze of the turtle's mind is destroyed before she can draw forth from it a single clear idea, the resolution of such crises of thinking in Book X is not always violent. In the well-known final poem, "Le Marchand, le gentilhomme, le pâtre, et le fils de roi," it will be the least prepossessing of these "chercheurs de nouveaux mondes," the herdsman, who finds the most useful means of coping with their distress. Instruction in arithmetic, politics, and heraldry ("ce jargon frivole") cannot assuage hunger. The herdsman chides his companions for proposing such pointless paths; when it is a question of putting food on the table, he tells them, "votre science / Est courte là-dessus: ma main y suppléera." In order to "conserver ses jours," concludes the narrator, "La main est le plus sûr et le plus prompt secours." Yet this lesson is by no means a fitting road-map for every labyrinth in the *Fables*. The hand of the human executioner in fable 1 gave no comfort to the snake, and no real threat was parried by this tyrannical use of power. The blind man in fable 9 who mistakes a serpent for a whip, despite a passerby's warning, perishes for allowing his hand to control his head. And the fabulist's ultimate sage, the "Solitaire," will advise: "Apprendre à se connaître est le premier des soins / Qu'impose à tous mortels la Majesté suprême" (XII, 29). Yet this ideal signifies little to those (like the snake in X, 1, or the lamb in I, 10) whose destiny depends wholly on someone else's definition of justice.

So the *Fables* themselves turn out to be the supreme labyrinth for the critic. Meandering happily in the heart of La Fontaine's knot of language, below its polished surface (a mirage of discursive intentionality), one is constantly reminded how elusive is a totally accurate blueprint to the intricate architecture of these marvelous poems. For the modern reader, Theseus as scholar, whose mind wanders amid the passageways of Book X, the very absence of Ariadne's thread (leading to the light of univocal meaning) is in itself significant: the farther one travels, the more one learns but also, paradoxically, the less one finally knows.

Pierre Malandain's insistence on the role played in the *Fables* by the motif of wind (a figure suggestive, one might add, of the plight of a wayfarer lost in a labyrinth) is relevant to a discussion of the architecture of Book X:

Le vent ouvre et ferme le livre I des *Fables*, bise glacée
interrompant soudain le chant de la cigale, aquilon vengeur
jetant à bas la superbe d'un chêne trop sûr de lui. Le signal
en est clair: la morale des *Fables* sera une morale du grand
air, ouverte aux grands mouvements de la vie et du
monde; elle tiendra compte de la diversité des situations,
du cycle des saisons, des caprices du sort. Elément d'ouver-
ture donc, quant au contenu, mais aussi élément de clôture,
puisqu'il en détermine d'emblée une dimension virtuelle.[16]

Combining the literal notion of wind as atmospheric force
with the metaphorical concept of winds of fortune, the
fabulist in poem 14 of Book X ("Discours à Monsieur le
Duc de La Rochefoucault") compares the behavior of humans with that of rabbits—to the detriment of the former:

> Dispersés par quelque orage,
> A peine ils touchent le port
> Qu'ils vont hasarder encor
> Même vent, même naufrage.
> Vrais lapins, on les revoit
> Sous les mains de la fortune.

In symbolic terms, the human race depicted here forsakes
the security of the liberating thread for the dangers of the
labyrinth; forfeiting the opportunity to learn from experience, these individuals place themselves without protest
under the hands of destiny (the rhyming of *mains* and
humains in the lines immediately preceding this heptasyllabic passage foreshadows their fate while highlighting a
key image of Book X).

It is wind as a physical phenomenon that has jeopardized the lives of the four adventurers in fable 15
("Quatre chercheurs de nouveaux mondes, / Presque nus
échappés à la fureur des ondes"), but in fable 9 the decent
shepherd at court narrowly averts an unpleasant fate in the
winds of political fortune: "Mainte peste de Cour fit tant,

par maint ressort, / Que la candeur du Juge, ainsi que son mérite, / Furent suspects au Prince." Elsewhere in Book X wind is verbiage or empty rhetoric: in fable 10 ("Les Poissons et le berger qui joue de la flûte"), a shepherd pronounces a "discours éloquent" to attract some fish into a treacherous enclosure ("Un vivier vous attend, plus clair que fin cristal": cf. poem 3) in order to please his beloved Annette, but his windy words return to their source ("ses paroles miellées / S'en étant aux vents envolées, / Il tendit un long rets"); in fable 11 ("Les Deux Perroquets, le roi, et son fils"), a father parrot, who has retaliated for the murder of his son by blinding the human prince responsible for the deed, fears becoming in his turn a victim in a chain of vengeance and is thus unpersuaded by the king's verbal offer of continued friendship ("prétends-tu par ta foi / Me leurrer de l'appât d'un profane langage?"); in fable 12 ("La Lionne et l'ourse"), the narrator, scornfully addressing the "Misérables humains" who, like the grieving mother lion who lost her cub to a hunter, complain that they have been singled out by fate for special punishment, exclaims, "Je n'entends résonner que des plaintes frivoles." La Fontaine's fondness for laughing at excessive or wasted language (cf. the narrator's comment in "La Jeune Veuve," VI, 21: "On fait beaucoup de bruit, et puis on se console") is reflected in Book X when, in his role as commentator on literary form, the fabulist explains why he will withhold information about the fortuitous uniting of the improbable quartet of travelers in poem 15 ("C'est un récit de longue haleine"); similarly, in fable 14 he decides to abridge a potentially long list of examples to "appuyer mon discours" because ". . . les ouvrages les plus courts / Sont toujours les meilleurs." But any careful reader of the *Fables* will be hard to convince that the poet really believed in the truth of a rule as inflexible as this one sounds. If short works are *always* the best, why has the fabulist inserted this judgment in a poem seventy lines long (the average length in the *deuxième recueil* being forty-six lines per poem)? He is not obliquely mocking his own prolixity, for in this very poem he calls attention even more pointedly to the need for brevity by declaring ". . . qu'il faut laisser / Dans les plus beaux sujets quelque chose à penser: / Ainsi ce discours doit cesser"; in other words, he has tried to make the fable as short as the circumstances permitted. Is it conceivable that La Fontaine, unaware of evidence his poems may supply, was persuaded that the typical fable in Books I–VI was demonstrably better as a work of art than the typical fable in Books VII–XI, the average poem in the 1678–79 collection being approximately fifty percent longer than its counterpart in the *Fables* of 1668?[17] Had this been his point of view, he would surely have abandoned his pen by the end of Book VII (or, depending on the time of composition, after writing a few of the expansive poems that characterize the *deuxième recueil*). If the rule of brevity is a basic law of Lafontainian composition, its applicability must be related to a consideration of context (the misleading adverb *toujours* notwithstanding); thus, in fable 9, the poet would gladly tell us how ambition succeeds in extending its "empire" if he did not have more pressing concerns ("mais mon but est de dire / Comme un Roi fit venir un Berger à sa Cour"). Like the inviting *vivier* of fable 10, deceptively termed "plus clair que fin cristal," the pellucid surface of declaration in La Fontaine must not allow the reader to forget that there always remains "quelque chose à penser" after the net worth of ostensibly straightforward statements has been determined. Whereas many of La Fontaine's ridiculous characters tend to spend their words lavishly, the poet in his narrative pose often substitutes for a prodigal surplus of speech what has been dubbed (by Jacques-Henri Périvier) the "esprit de litote."

The motley cast of Book X, trapped in a variety of labyrinths, offers ample evidence of the possible effects of words unwisely used, chatter out of control, expression surpassing the bounds of necessity or propriety. Unlike the man in fable 1 who, though less eloquent (ironically) than the beasts and tree opposing him, mutters his ill-founded verdict with impunity, the vain turtle in fable 2 dies as a result of uttering a speech both pointless and poorly timed; hearing herself proclaimed "la Reine des Tortues," she foolishly acknowledges the compliment:

> Car lâchant le bâton en desserrant les dents,
> Elle tombe, elle crève aux pieds des regardants.
> Son indiscrétion de sa perte fut cause.
> Imprudence, babil, et sotte vanité,
>   Et vaine curiosité,
>   Ont ensemble étroit parentage.
> Ce sont enfants tous d'un lignage.

The treachery of her tongue links the tortoise phonologically (though not etymologically) with the aging bird of fable 3 who "Souffrait une disette extrême." Having spoken at a disastrously inopportune moment, the turtle is ridiculed because she has used language as an instrument of self-destruction. In the first place, she invited her fatal predicament when she "Communiqua ce beau dessein" (to travel abroad) to the two ducks; had she held her tongue, the circumstances leading to her personal disaster would not have materialized. When she decided to unclench her teeth in order to reveal her ambition, she was already courting trouble, but she could not yet imagine the grave implications of the expression *desserrer les dents*. The poet insists doubly here on the vanity of the tortoise: her "sotte vanité" is coupled with her "vaine curiosité." As David Lee Rubin has indicated, *vaine* and *vanité* are to be read here "in their usual sense, which refers to pride and futility, and [also] in their etymological sense, which refers to emptiness" (*Higher, Hidden Order*, p. 20). In addition, *vaine* can suggest *légère* or *illusoire* as well as *faible* or *épuisée* (*NDE*, p. 780): the absurdly dangerous curiosity of the turtle is a vivid example of her "tête légère" in action;

the prospect of exciting travel to exotic lands will turn out
to be a tragically enticing mirage; her acceptance of the
ducks' proposal is a fitting illustration of her feckless, exhausted intellect (the breeding ground of her mindless
utterances). The manner of her death is in perfect harmony
with the flaws in her personality ("elle crève"). As Rubin
judiciously states:

> "Crever" means not only to die but to burst, and upon
> bursting, a turtle's shell releases its contents and becomes
> empty. The turtle thus suffers punishment in the image of
> her defect: for vacuousness, she becomes a void. (p. 20)

This turtle may have had a hollow mind in the image of
her now-empty shell, but it would be unwise to conclude
with Alain-Marie Bassy (who uses this poem to illustrate
the point) that "Tout voyageur n'est, pour La Fontaine,
qu'un vaniteux et un imprudent" ("*Fables*": *La Fontaine*, p.
94), because the astonishing success of one of the soldiers
of fortune in fable 13 ("Les Deux Aventuriers et le talis-
man"), proclaimed monarch after carrying an elephant to
the top of a mountain (in accordance with the strange
advice he had found written on a placard), moves the
fabulist to conclude:

> Fortune aveugle suit aveugle hardiesse.
> Le sage quelquefois fait bien d'exécuter,
> Avant que de donner le temps à la sagesse
> D'envisager le fait, et sans la consulter.

The key word here is *quelquefois:* the narrator offers a
promising clue for locating a safe exit from the maze of
puzzling alternatives for a given course of action, but as
the reader gropes for the thread it is hastily withdrawn.
For the *Fables* are not a guidebook to human conduct. If
La Fontaine had really taken seriously the business of
philosophizing, it is most unlikely that he would have
chosen to express his ideas in heterometric rhymed verse.

Stumbling through the esthetic labyrinth of the *Fables* is essentially a game with hidden rules that the reader agrees to play with the master ironist who, in command of the pen, can draw new passageways wherever he decides while sealing others.

The double reference to lack of sight in the passage quoted above ("Fortune aveugle suit aveugle hardiesse") underscores the preoccupation in Book X with real, virtual, or figurative blindness, a notion evocative of the situation of individuals walking aimlessly in a labyrinth. When the fortunate adventurer in fable 13 embarks on his mission he dashes off "Les yeux clos." Unblessed with good luck, on the other hand, is the literally blind man of fable 9 who, ignoring the passerby's warning about the "animal traître et pernicieux" he is holding ("L'aveugle enfin ne le crut pas"), learns too late that the serpent he had found numb with cold is not merely a stiffened lash ("Il en perdit bientôt la vie"). Whereas the cormorant of fable 3, "un peu trop vieux pour voir au fond des eaux," learns how to cope with his weakened eyesight, the future of the prince in fable 11 is left unreported from the moment when the father parrot pecks out his eyes. Numerous characters in Book X are metaphorically blind: the man in fable 1, for example, who fails to accept the well-reasoned indictment of his own conduct; the voyaging turtle "à la tête légère" in fable 2; the fish in fable 3, who pay a heavy price for the lesson that "l'on ne doit jamais avoir de confiance / En ceux qui sont mangeurs de gens"; the greedy *compère* in fable 4, whom the reformed miser cleverly teaches that "Il n'est pas malaisé de tromper un trompeur"; the humans in fable 5, who simple-mindedly adopt a double standard when judging their own behavior and that of the wolf; the spider in fable 6, whose head and feet become "artisans superflus" when she finds herself the swallow's prisoner (she had been portrayed as blind to nature's rule of superior force); the dog "Mouflar" in fable 8, who is at first unaware that having his ears clipped can be less a liability than a tactical advantage ("il vit avec le temps / Qu'il y gagnait beaucoup"); the shepherd in fable 10, confidently unmindful that honeyed speech is no substitute for force ("la puissance fait tout"; his figurative ailment is comically mirrored by that of the fish who ignore his "discours éloquent": "L'auditoire était sourd aussi bien que muet"); the narrator in fable 14, who *appears* to be confidently unaware that his own behavior resembles that of countless characters from Book I onward whose unjust appropriation of power over others he has mocked, frequently with the weapons of understatement ("Et nouveau Jupiter du haut de cet olympe, / Je foudroie, à discrétion, / Un lapin qui n'y pensait guère"); and the merchant, gentleman, and prince in fable 15, who would have floundered in intellectual pursuits if the herdsman had not shown them how to deal pragmatically with their immediate predicament—the need to avoid starvation. But not everyone in the *Fables* is in a position to follow his advice, which is expressed elsewhere (VI, 18) as "Aide-toi, le Ciel t'aidera." A solution that stands the test of events in one context is likely to be subverted in another.

I hope these remarks (which by no means exhaust the subject) help establish the importance of the labyrinth, narrowly and broadly defined, as a means of understanding the ironic architecture of Book X. But these poems could be approached from other angles as well. It seems to me that any attempt to organize these fables along thematic, philosophical, or political lines is likely to leave their texture virtually untouched; thus Georges Couton's three-part division of the poems of Book X (see above) and Pierre Bornecque's distribution of its themes into five categories[18] appear to becloud the subjacent architecture of the unit. More instructive, I believe, would be a close analysis of the functions of corporal imagery (especially the roles played by hand, head, eyes, and mouth), the introduction from poem to poem of character types who reappear as the title personages in fable 15, the interweaving of mythological references with images of death and domination, or a consideration of Book X as illustrative of La Fontaine's vertical imagination (in this book real or implicit rising and falling abound). It might likewise be profitable to pursue Philip A. Wadsworth's suggestion (made in a personal letter dated 22 July 1982) to begin a study of Book X with the "Discours à Madame de La Sablière" at the end of Book IX. In any event, much careful investigation of La Fontaine's elusive architectural patterns deserves to be undertaken.

NOTES

1. "The Art of Transition in La Fontaine," in his *Essays on Seventeenth-Century French Literature,* ed. and trans. David Bellos (Cambridge: Cambridge Univ. Press, 1983), pp. 169–207; originally pub. as "Die Kunst des Übergangs bei La Fontaine," *PMLA,* 53 (1938), 393–433; rpt. in French as "L'Art de la transition chez La Fontaine" in *Etudes de style* (Paris: Gallimard, 1970), pp. 166–207.
2. *Young La Fontaine: A Study of His Artistic Growth in His Early Poetry and First Fables* (Evanston: Northwestern Univ. Press, 1952), p. 215.
3. *Thèmes et variations dans le premier recueil des "Fables" de La Fontaine (1668),* Les Cours de Sorbonne (Paris: Centre de Documentation Universitaire, 1960).
4. See his meticulously researched two-volume study, *La Fontaine et le premier recueil des "Fables,"* to which I referred earlier.
5. In *La Fontaine fabuliste,* cited in chapter III; and also in *"Fables": La Fontaine,* Profil d'une Oeuvre, 67 (Paris: Hatier, 1979).
6. See *Le Monde littéraire de La Fontaine,* pp. 163–226.
7. See *La Fontaine fabuliste,* pp. 89–102.
8. "Le Livre épicurien des *Fables:* Essai de lecture du livre VIII," *Travaux de Linguistique et de Littérature Publiés par le Cen-*

tre de Philologie et de Littératures Romanes de l'Université de Strasbourg, 13, No. 2 (1975), 283–90.

9. "Remarques sur la disposition par livres des *Fables* de La Fontaine," in *De Jean Lemaire de Belges à Jean Giraudoux: Mélanges d'histoire et de critique littéraire offerts à Pierre Jourda* (Paris: Nizet, 1970), pp. 227–48.

10. Gross, "Order and Theme in La Fontaine's *Fables,* Book VI," *L'Esprit Créateur,* 21, No. 4 (Winter 1981), 78–89; Danner, "La Fontaine's *Fables,* Book X: The Labyrinth Hypothesis," *L'Esprit Créateur,* 21, No. 4 (Winter 1981), 90–98. Most of the substance of my article concerning the labyrinth reappears in the present chapter.

11. *La Fable et l'intertexte,* Collection ENTAILLE/S (Paris: Temps Actuels, 1981), p. 72.

12. *"Fables": La Fontaine:* (Paris: Hatier, 1973).

13. I am inclined to agree with Philip A. Wadsworth, who argues modestly that this fable is "tout simplement un épilogue à la fin du douzième livre," placed there by a poet eager to "réussir un beau final." See "Le Douzième Livre des Fables," pp. 111–15.

14. Henri Lafay recently published an essay on the problem of *parole* in this fable: " 'L'Homme et la couleuvre' ou la parole de La Fontaine: Analyse de fonctionnement textuel," in *Mélanges offerts à Georges Couton* (Lyon: Presses Universitaires de Lyon, 1981), pp. 371–82. For Lafay, ". . . c'est tout le texte de la fable qui est toujours parole et parole ambiguë, de son appartenance même à la fable. Car la fable parle sans cesse: c'en est l'essence; ses figures existent de leur dessein de plaire, certes, mais en même temps de dire (instruire). Et elles fonctionnent comme masques, masques pour cacher et masques pour laisser voir, parce que la fable est métaphorique et que la métaphore est un langage au moins double" (p. 377).

15. See David Lee Rubin's brief but cogent analysis of this fable in *Higher, Hidden Order: Design and Meaning in the Odes of Malherbe* (Chapel Hill: Univ. of North Carolina Press, 1972), pp. 20–21. Rubin's semantic discussion of such key terms as *légère, vanité,* and *crever* meshes nicely with the mind-as-labyrinth supposition.

16. *La Fable et l'intertexte,* p. 73; see his discussion of wind as a case of "fonctionnement intratextuel," pp. 71–80.

17. This statistical comparison is based on line counts found in Bornecque, *La Fontaine fabuliste,* p. 79.

18. Bornecque perceives this ordering of "cinq thèmes entrelacés" in Book X: "le cycle de l'aventure" (fables 2, 13, 15); "le cycle de la mise en accusation de l'homme par les bêtes et par les plantes" (fables 1, 5, 7, 8); "le cycle de l'avidité" (fables 3, 4, 6); "le cycle de la condition royale" (fables 9, 10, 11, 12); "le thème du comportement identique des hommes et des bêtes" (fable 14): *La Fontaine fabuliste,* pp. 100–01. This classification depends heavily on extraliterary typologies and fails to exploit, for instance, the *language* of royalty (e.g., the title "Reine des Tortues" falsely conferred on the turtle in fable 2; the disparaged humans—"rois des animaux, ou plutôt leurs tyrans"—in fable 8) or the transcendent royalty of Jupiter, destiny, or providence, invoked in a number of these poems.

Conclusion

My approach to the *Fables* (or, for that matter, to any literary work) is informed by the deeply held belief that it is much more satisfying, both intellectually and affectively, to look for the qualities that have enabled the poetry (or theater, or fiction) to survive—and thrive—than to become preoccupied with issues (however worthy of examination on other grounds) that increase the distance between the reader and the literary text. Thus, for instance, in reading the works of La Fontaine I find that knowledge of how this or that poem is perhaps covertly connected to some episode in the Fouquet-Colbert controversy will in no way enhance my appreciation of the poem as an esthetically enduring artifact. Nor will speculations about the fabulist's possible private attitudes toward women or children or royalty enable me to decide why it is worthwhile to take the time to read and slowly reread his poetry in the final quarter of the twentieth century. Although irony is by no means the only viable access route into the magical territory of the *Fables*, in the preceding chapters I have attempted to demonstrate that La Fontaine's ironic outlook, precisely defined, can be seen to permeate a wide array of poems, and that his ironic imagination has contributed much to the artistically vibrant, ageless qualities that one quickly senses when perusing almost any Lafontainian fable.

I trust that those who disagree with my reading of the *Fables* will at least judge my approach worthy of being debated, because few are more forlorn than the critic whom no one chooses to cite—either to concur or to dispute.

To those who are more or less in agreement with my position that irony lies at the very center of our fabulist's art, I would like to suggest several directions for future inquiry. In the first place, a full study might be profitably devoted to interrelationships between didactic elements in the *Fables* and La Fontaine's ironic artistry. Of great usefulness in this regard would no doubt be a careful consideration of David H. Richter's classification of apologues and his distinctions between types of apologues (or "rhetorical fictions") and "represented actions" (as explained in *Fable's End*). And what might the seeker of irony learn from the continual ebb and flow of Epicurean concepts throughout the *Fables?* Would a systematic study of all twelve books reveal a fabulist bent on undermining, meticulously albeit clandestinely, the traditional apologue's ostensible power to teach? If so, to what extent would literary historians be obliged to alter their assessment of the poet's implied world-view?

Another profitable angle of access to the *Fables* might well be the development of a taxonomy of La Fontaine's ironic strategies, beginning in effect where Jean Dominique Biard's indispensable book on the style of the *Fables* ended, and profiting fully from his penetrating discoveries. Ideally, such a study would move well beyond classification in order to provide a coherent overview of La Fontaine's lasting contributions to the craft of irony in literature.

Finally, my approach to the architecture of Book X could perhaps be advantageously applied to every book of the *Fables*, with variations to allow for the uniqueness of the aggregate subject matter of each unit. One can hope that the ultimate result of this kind of work would be a considerably amplified awareness of the fabulist's artistic master plan: that is, the structural and textural design of the *Fables*, conceived and actualized by the (implied) author as he reveals himself through the poetic texts.

Such research efforts, whatever their exegetical successes or shortcomings on balance, would have (minimally) one strong and undeniable merit: they would be, as

Wayne C. Booth says of his own study of irony, "una-bashedly in a tradition of evangelical attempts to save the world, or at least a piece of it, through critical attention to language" (*A Rhetoric of Irony*, p. xii). The undying heritage the world has acquired from Jean de La Fontaine is the language of his literary corpus, and we still have much to learn about how and what his works may be trying to communicate to us. If this book has managed to shed even a few rays of light on the language of the *Fables* by summoning from across the centuries a poet's profoundly ironic voice and fathoming some of its faintly perceptible resonances, it will have served a useful purpose.

Selected Bibliography

A. Works by La Fontaine: Short List of Useful Modern Editions

Oeuvres complètes. 2 vols. Bibliothèque de la Pléiade. Paris: Gallimard, 1954, 1958. (Vol. 1, edited by René Groos and Jacques Schiffrin, contains the *Fables* as well as the *Contes et nouvelles;* vol. 2, edited by Pierre Clarac, contains the *Oeuvres diverses.)*

Fables. Ed. René Radouant. New ed. Paris: Hachette, 1929.

Fables choisies mises en vers. Ed. Georges Couton. Classiques Garnier. Paris: Garnier, 1962.

Fables. Ed. Pierre Michel and Maurice Martin. 2 vols. Petits Classiques Bordas. Paris: Bordas, 1964.

Contes et nouvelles en vers. Ed. Georges Couton. Classiques Garnier. Paris: Garnier, 1961.

B. Books and Articles on La Fontaine

Barchilon, Jacques. "Wit and Humor in La Fontaine's *Psyché." French Review,* 36 (1962), 23–31.

Bassy, Alain-Marie. *"Fables":* La Fontaine. Collection Thema/*anthologie.* Paris: Hatier, 1973.

Baudin, Emile. *La Philosophie morale des "Fables" de La Fontaine.* Neuchâtel: Editions de la Baconnière, 1951.

Beugnot, Bernard. "Autour d'un texte: L'Ultime Leçon des *Fables." Travaux de Linguistique et de Littérature Publiés par le Centre de Philologie et de Littératures Romanes de l'Université de Strasbourg,* 13, No. 2 (1975), 291–301.

Biard, Jean Dominique. *The Style of La Fontaine's Fables.* New York: Barnes & Noble, 1966.

Blavier-Paquot, Simone. *La Fontaine: Vues sur l'art du moraliste dans les "Fables" de 1668.* Paris: Société d'Edition "Les Belles Lettres," 1961.

Bornecque, Pierre. *La Fontaine fabuliste.* Paris: Société d'Edition d'Enseignement Supérieur, 1973.

———. *"Fables": La Fontaine.* Profil d'une Oeuvre, 67. Paris: Hatier, 1979.

Bray, René. *Les Fables de La Fontaine.* 1929; rpt. Paris: Nizet, 1946.

Brody, Jules. "Irony in La Fontaine: From Message to Massage." *Papers on French Seventeenth Century Literature,* No. 11 (1979), pp. 77–89.

Clarac, Pierre. "Variations de La Fontaine dans les six derniers livres des *Fables.*" *L'Information Littéraire,* Jan.–Feb. 1951, pp. 1–9.

———. *La Fontaine.* Nouv. éd. revue et corrigée. Connaissance des Lettres, 21. Paris: Hatier, 1959.

———. *La Fontaine par lui-même.* Ecrivains de Toujours. Paris: Editions du Seuil, 1961.

Coates, Carrol F. "Poetic Technique and Meaning in La Fontaine's *Fables.*" In *Studies in Romance Languages and Literatures.* Ed. Sandra M. Cypess. Lawrence, KS: Coronado Press, 1979, pp. 62–76.

Collinet, Jean-Pierre. *Le Monde littéraire de La Fontaine.* Paris: Presses Universitaires de France, 1970.

Couton, Georges. *La Poétique de La Fontaine.* Paris: Presses Universitaires de France, 1957.

———. *La Politique de La Fontaine.* Paris: Société d'Edition "Les Belles Lettres," 1959.

———. "Le Livre épicurien des *Fables:* Essai de lecture du livre VIII." *Travaux de Linguistique et de Littérature Publiés par le Centre de Philologie et de Littératures Romanes de l'Université de Strasbourg,* 13, No. 2 (1975), 283–90.

Danner, G. Richard. "Individualism in La Fontaine's 'Le Loup et le chien.'" *Kentucky Romance Quarterly,* 24 (1977), 185–90.

_____. "La Fontaine's Ironic Vision in the *Fables*." *French Review*, 50 (1977), 562–71.

_____. "Selection and Sacrifice in La Fontaine's 'Le Satyre et le passant.' " *Papers on French Seventeenth Century Literature*, No. 8 (Winter 1977–78), 196–207.

_____. "La Fontaine's 'Compagnons d'Ulysse': The Merits of Metamorphosis." *French Review*, 53 (1980), 239–47.

_____. "La Fontaine's *Fables*, Book X: The Labyrinth Hypothesis." *L'Esprit Créateur*, 21, No. 4 (Winter 1981), 90–98.

_____. "Jean de La Fontaine." In *European Writers: The Age of Reason and the Enlightenment*. Ed. George Stade. New York: Charles Scribner's Sons, 1984, III, 73–100.

Gohin, Ferdinand. *L'Art de La Fontaine dans ses "Fables."* Bibliothèque d'Histoire Littéraire et de Critique. Paris: Garnier, 1929.

_____. *La Fontaine, études et recherches.* Paris: Garnier, 1937.

Gross, Nathan. "Order and Theme in La Fontaine's *Fables*, Book VI." *L'Esprit Créateur*, 21, No. 4 (Winter 1981), 78–89.

Guiton, Margaret. *La Fontaine: Poet and Counterpoet.* New Brunswick, NJ: Rutgers Univ. Press, 1961.

Gutwirth, Marcel. "Le Chêne et le Roseau, ou les cheminements de la mimésis." *French Review*, 48 (1975), 695–702.

Haig, Stirling. "La Fontaine's 'Le Loup et le chien' as a Pedagogical Instrument." *French Review*, 42 (1969), 701–05.

Hytier, Jean. "La Vocation lyrique de La Fontaine." *French Studies*, 25 (1971), 136–55.

Jasinski, René. "Sur la philosophie de La Fontaine dans les livres VII à XII des *Fables*." *Revue d'His-

toire de la Philosophie, NS 1 (1933), 316–30; NS 2 (1934), 218–42.

_____. *La Fontaine et le premier recueil des "Fables."* 2 vols. Paris: Nizet, 1965–66.

Kohn, Renée. *Le Goût de La Fontaine.* Paris: Presses Universitaires de France, 1962.

Lafay, Henri. "'L'Homme et la couleuvre' ou la parole de La Fontaine: Analyse de fonctionnement textuel." In *Mélanges offerts à Georges Couton.* Lyon: Presses Universitaires de Lyon, 1981, pp. 371–82.

Lapp, John C. *The Esthetics of Negligence: La Fontaine's Contes.* Cambridge: Cambridge Univ. Press, 1971.

Lyons, John D. "Author and Reader in the *Fables.*" *French Review,* 49 (1975), 59–67.

Malandain, Pierre. *La Fable et l'intertexte.* Collection ENTAILLE/S. Paris: Temps Actuels, 1981.

Merino-Morais, Jane. *Différence et répétition dans les "Contes" de La Fontaine.* Gainesville: University Presses of Florida, 1983.

Michaut, Gustave. *La Fontaine.* 2 vols. 1912–14; rpt. Paris: Hachette, 1929.

Moreau, Pierre. *Thèmes et variations dans le premier recueil des "Fables" de La Fontaine (1668).* Les Cours de Sorbonne. Paris: Centre de Documentation Universitaire, 1960.

Mourgues, Odette de. *La Fontaine: Fables.* London: Edward Arnold, 1960.

_____. *O muse, fuyante proie: Essai sur la poésie de La Fontaine.* Paris: José Corti, 1962.

Périvier, Jacques-Henri. "'La Cigale et la fourmi' comme introduction aux *Fables.*" *French Review,* 42 (1969), 418–27.

_____. "Fondement et mode de l'éthique dans les *Fables* de La Fontaine." *Kentucky Romance Quarterly,* 18 (1971), 333–42.

Proust, Jacques. "Remarques sur la disposition par livres des *Fables* de La Fontaine." In *Mélanges d'histoire et de critique littéraire offerts à Pierre Jourda*. Paris: Nizet, 1971.

Richard, Noël. *La Fontaine et les "Fables" du deuxième recueil*. Paris: Nizet, 1972.

Rubin, David Lee. *Higher, Hidden Order: Design and Meaning in the Odes of Malherbe*. Chapel Hill: Univ. of North Carolina Press, 1972, pp. 20–21.

————. "Four Modes of Double Irony in La Fontaine's *Fables*." In *The Equilibrium of Wit: Essays for Odette de Mourgues*. Ed. Peter Bayley and Dorothy Gabe Coleman. Lexington, KY: French Forum, Publishers, 1982, pp. 201–12.

Runte, Roseann. "Narrator and Reader: Keys to Irony in La Fontaine." *Australian Journal of French Studies*, 16 (1979), 389–400.

Spitzer, Leo. "Die Kunst des Übergangs bei La Fontaine." *PMLA*, 53 (1938), 393–433. Rpt. in English as "The Art of Transition in La Fontaine" in Leo Spitzer, *Essays on Seventeenth-Century French Literature*. Ed. and trans. David Bellos. Cambridge: Cambridge Univ. Press, 1983, pp. 169–207.

Tiefenbrun, Susan W. "Signs of Irony in La Fontaine's *Fables*." In her *Signs of the Hidden: Semiotic Studies*. Amsterdam: Rodopi, 1980, pp. 143–61.

————. "The Art and Artistry of Teaching in the *Fables* of La Fontaine." *L'Esprit Créateur*, 21, No. 4 (Winter 1981), 50–65.

Tyler, J. Allen. *A Concordance to the Fables and Tales of Jean de La Fontaine*. Ithaca: Cornell Univ. Press, 1974.

Wadsworth, Philip A. *Young La Fontaine: A Study of His Artistic Growth in His Early Poetry and First Fables*. Evanston, IL: Northwestern Univ. Press, 1952.

_____. "La Fontaine's Theories on the Fable as a Literary Form." *Rice University Studies*, 57, No. 2 (Spring 1971), 115–27.

_____. "The Art of Allegory in La Fontaine's *Fables*." *French Review*, 45 (1972), 1125–35.

_____. "Le Douzième Livre des *Fables*." *Cahiers de l'Association Internationale des Etudes Françaises*, No. 26 (May 1974), pp. 103–15.

_____. "Smiling with La Fontaine." *Papers on French Seventeenth Century Literature*, No. 13 (1980), pp. 291–308.

Youssef, Zobeidah. *La Poésie de l'eau dans les "Fables" de La Fontaine*. Biblio 17, 3. Paris: Papers on French Seventeenth Century Literature, 1981.

C. Literary Theory: Short List of Relevant Works

Booth, Wayne C. *A Rhetoric of Irony*. Chicago: Univ. of Chicago Press, 1974.

Frye, Northrop. *Anatomy of Criticism: Four Essays*. Princeton: Princeton Univ. Press, 1957.

Hirsch, E. D., Jr. *Validity in Interpretation*. New Haven: Yale Univ. Press, 1967.

Jankélévitch, Vladimir. *L'Ironie*. Paris: Flammarion, 1964.

Muecke, D. C. *The Compass of Irony*. London: Methuen, 1969.

_____. *Irony and the Ironic*. 2nd ed. The Critical Idiom, 13. London: Methuen, 1982.

Olson, Elder. *The Theory of Comedy*. Bloomington: Indiana Univ. Press, 1968.

Richter, David H. *Fable's End: Completeness and Closure in Rhetorical Fiction*. Chicago: Univ. of Chicago Press, 1974.

Smith, Barbara Herrnstein. *Poetic Closure: A Study of How Poems End*. Chicago: Univ. of Chicago Press, 1968.

Thompson, Allan Reynolds. *The Dry Mock: A Study of Irony in Drama.* Berkeley: Univ. of California Press, 1948.

Wellek, René, and Austin Warren. *Theory of Literature.* 3rd ed. New York: Harcourt, Brace & World, 1956.

Index